COUNTY FOLK-LORE
Printed extracts no. 3.

LEICESTERSHIRE
& RUTLAND

The Folklore Society, original publishers of this book, was founded in 1878 and was the first learned society in the world to be devoted to the study of folklore. Its expressed aims were to encourage research and collection of traditional culture, and to make the results of this research available to scholars and the public at large.

The Society is still going strong, and organises regular conferences and other events, issues a well-respected journal and members' newsletter, publishes books on folklore topics, and maintains an extensive library and archive service which is based in University College London. Membership is open to anyone interested in furthering the Society's aims.

Information regarding the Society's activities and current subscription rates is available from The Folklore Society, University College London, Gower Street, London WC1E 6BT (Tel 071 387 5894).

Facsimile reprint 1997
LLANERCH PUBLISHERS
Felinfach

ISBN 1 86143 034 5

Issued by the FOLK-LORE SOCIETY.]

COUNTY FOLK-LORE.

PRINTED EXTRACTS, No. 3.

LEICESTERSHIRE & RUTLAND.

COLLECTED AND EDITED

BY

CHARLES JAMES BILLSON, M.A.

Facsimile reprint 1997
LLANERCH PUBLISHERS/FOLKLORE SOCIETY

Published for the Folk-Lore Society by
D. NUTT, 270, STRAND, W.C.

1895.

INTRODUCTION

The word "folklore" was invented almost 150 years ago, on August 22 1846, when the antiquarian W. J. Thoms appealed in the *Athenæum* for readers to join in recording"... what we in England designate as Popular Antiquities or Popular Literature (though by-the-by it is more a Lore than a Literature, and would be most aptly described by a good Saxon compound, Folk-lore) ...". The word was new, but the subject was not; for two hundred years antiquarians had been fascinated by local and seasonal customs, popular tales, traditions, beliefs which did not conform to official relligion or science. Such material appears sporadically in the writings of William Camden (1551-1623), and far more abundantly in those of John Aubrey (1626-97). Some decades later came Henry Bourne's *Antiquitates Vulgares* (1725), a fierce attack against popular relligious observances such as Christmas carols or visiting holy wells, because they were originally Roman Catholic, "the invention of indolent monks", and so undoubtedly diabolical and heathen. His book, ignored at the time, was incorporated in 1777 into a much larger and more influential work, John Brand's *Observations on Popular Antiquities*. Brand agreed that most folk customs dated from before the Reformation, but he was free from the Puritan intolerance which equated Catholicism with paganism, and he enjoyed historical research for its own sake. He went on gathering material till his death in 1806, mostly by copying from books and journals, but sometimes by personal observation. After he died, his book was reissued in a greatly enlarged edition, incorporating the later notes by Henry Ellis (1815). It had grown into a vast, confused scrapbook: local historians pounced upon it and used it as a model for their own researches.

In the course of the nineteenth century, many

scholars boldly tried to formulate some all-embracing theory which would explain the origin and significance of myths, folktales, superstitions and magical beliefs, and the more picturesque folk customs, especially those connected with agriculture. The explanations offered went far beyond medieval Catholicism. Some suggested origins in pre-Christian Germanic or Celtic cultures; others, noting similarities with beliefs and rituals found among "primitive" non-European peoples, argued that folklore consisted of survivals from a prehistoric "savage" stage in human social development. The debate between these and other conflicting theories was carried on energetically at a high scholarly level, and attracted much public interest. It has been well described in Richard M. Dorson's The British Folklorists: A History (1968). And although modern scholars agree that all these Victorian attempts to find "a key to all mythologies" ended in failure, due to oversimplifications of the highly complex topics, some of the theories then launched are still to be found recycled in popular form: prehistoric paganism and Celtic paganism, separately or combined, are currently enjoying a fashionable revival in the mass market.

By the 1890s the Folklore Society, which had been founded in 1878, saw a need for systematic and accurate documentation of traditions within specific localities: huge unwieldy compilations like Brand's would not do. Between 1895 and 1914 seven volumes of County Folklore: Printed Extracts were published by the Society. The first covered three counties: Gloucestershire by E. S. Hartland, Suffolk by Lady Carilla Eveline Gurdon, and Leicestershire and Rutland by C. J. Billson. The rest covered one region apiece: The North Riding of Yorkshire, York, and the Ainsty by Eliza Gutch; Orkney and Shetland Islands by George Black, and ed. N. W. Thomas; Northumberland by M. C. Balfour and N. W. Thomas; Lincolnshire by Eliza

Gutch and Mabel Peacock; The East Riding of Yorkshire by Eliza Gutch; and Fife by J. E. Simpkins. The
1914 war then interrupted the project.

These books may seem strange today because, like
Brand's, they consist almost entirely of extracts from
previously printed books and journals. Fieldwork, i.e.
gathering information through interviews or by tape-
recording, filming, and personal observation, is central
to a present-day folklorist's technique, and was already
practised in Victorian times by means of the simple
notebook. Yet from these books it is virtually absent;
editorial theorising and interpretation are also minimal.
It must be stressed that the "Printed Extracts" series
was never intended to stand alone, but to be a starting
point for further study of the contemporary lore of
each area. In his preface to the Gloucestershire volume, Hartland made "suggestions for systematic collection of folklore" to be undertaken by university
students, school teachers, clergy, doctors, local historians and others. Plenty of his contemporaries were
already working in this way; the purpose of reprinting
old material was to provide historical perspectives and
a set of securely dated benchmarks, from which to
measure later developments, innovations or loses.

Another century has passed, and the County Folk-
lore series is being reprinted in the 1990s, a period of
nostalgia for an idealized rural past, seen as a time of
idyllic simplicity and closeness to nature. Readers will
find ample encouragement for nostalgia here - picturesque accounts of harvest customs, Christmas customs,
fairs and festivals; old tales of ghosts, giants, fairies,
boggarts, witches, heroes, bandits, healing charms,
divinations, omens, spells; customs at marriage, birth
or death. It is only too easy to see in all this mere
quaintness and charm. To get a more historically bal-
anced picture one needs to remember also the harsh
social and economic conditions affecting very many

rural workers: one may well wonder, for instance, whether a good harvest supper really compensated for low wages during the other 51 weeks of the year. The "printed extracts", like old photographs, offer facts – but facts selected and presented according to the viewpoint of the observers who recorded them. Now, in the 1990s, we inevitably add interpretative viewpoints of our own, conditioned by the cultural assumptions of our age.

Folklore is an ongoing process, in which every custom, story or belief (if it survives) is constantly remodelled by social pressures so that it remains in some way relevant to changing conditions. Books written a hundred or two hundred years ago are in no sense a final word on the topic, nor are the versions of a story or custom which they contain necessarily "better" than the current ones – they merely pinpoint what it was like in one phase of its existence. Moreover, anything that is passed on through oral tradition exists in multiple versions, each differing in some degree from the next, and each equally valid. What is the "true" story about that haunted tree? What is the "right" way to dispose of Christmas decorations, and on what date? What "should" children do at Halloween? Are black cats lucky (UK), or unlucky (USA)? We shall never find definitive answers to such questions, but it is fascinating to compile our own observations about them, and to compare with writers who went hunting along the same tracks long before us.

Jacqueline Simpson,
President,
The Folklore Society,
February, 1994.

CONTENTS.

LIST OF AUTHORITIES.

A Flora of Leicestershire. By Mary Kirby. 1850.

A History of Guthlaxton Deaneries and adjacent Parishes. By the Rev. C. Holme. 1891.

An Essay on English Municipal History. By James Thompson. London. 1867.

Aubrey. "Remaines of Gentilisme." Folk-Lore Society. 1880.

Black, W. G. Folk Medicine. Folk-Lore Society. 1883.

Blore, Thomas. "The History and Antiquities of the County of Rutland." 1811.

Brand's "Popular Antiquities." 3 vols. London (Bohn). 1890.

Burton, William. "The Description of Leicestershire." 1622.

Bygone England. W. Andrews. 1892.

Bygone Leicestershire. W. Andrews. 1892.

Chambers's "Book of Days." 2 vols. 1864.

Dyer's "British Popular Customs." (Bohn.) 1876.

English Folk Rhymes. By G. F. Northall. London. 1892.

Evans, A. B. "Leicestershire Words, Phrases, and Proverbs." (Ed. Sebastian Evans.) 1881.

Folk-Lore and Provincial Names of British Birds. By the Rev. C. Swainson. London : Folk-Lore Society. 1886.

Folk-Lore Record.

Folk-Lore Journal.

Folk-Lore.

Gentleman's Magazine Library. 4 vols. "Popular Superstitions," 1884 ; "English Traditions," 1885 ; "Manners and Customs," 1883 ; "Dialect Proverb Word-lore, 1884.

Gipsy Sorcery and Fortune Telling. By C. G. Leland. London. 1892.

LIST OF AUTHORITIES.

Gomme, G. L. " Folk-Lore Relics of Early Village Life." 1883.

Gomme, G. L. " Primitive Folk-Moots." 1880.

Gomme, Mrs. " Traditional Games." Vol. I. 1894.

Grose, F. " Provincial Glossary." 1811.

Henderson, W. " Folk-Lore of the Northern Counties." Folk-Lore Society. 1879.

" *Holy Wells*," *their Legends and Superstitions*, by R. C. Hope, F.S.A., F.R.S.A. London : Elliott Stock. 1893.

Kelly, Wm. " Notices relating to the Drama, etc., Sixteenth and Seventeenth Centuries." 1865.

Leicester Journal.

Leicestershire Chronicle.

Leicester Daily Post.

Leicestershire Notes and Queries.

Macaulay, Rev. A. " History of Claybrook." 1791.

Music and Friends. By William Gardiner. 3 vols. 1838.

Naology ; or a Treatise on the Origin, Progress, and Symbolical Import of The Sacred Structures of the Most Eminent Nations and Ages of the World. By John Dudley, M.A., Vicar of Humberston and of Sileby, Leicestershire. London. 1846.

National Tales and Legends. W. C. Hazlitt. 1892.

Nichols' " History of Leicestershire." 4 vols. in 8, fol. 1795-1811.

North, Thomas. " Church Bells of Leicestershire." Leicester. 1876.

North, Thomas. " Chronicle of the Church of Saint Martin." 1866.

North, Thomas. " The Church Bells of Rutland." 1880.

Notes and Queries. " Choice Notes (Folk-Lore)." 1859.

Potter, T. R. " History of Charnwood Forest." 4to. 1842.

Ray's " English Proverbs." 4th Edition. 1768.

Royal Progresses and Visits to Leicester. By William Kelly, F.S.A., F.R.H.S. Leicester. 1884.

The Parish Records of Market Harborough. By the Rev. J. E. Stocks and W. B. Bragg. London. 1890.

Thompson, J. " History of Leicester to end of Eighteenth Century." 2 vols. 1849-71.

Throsby's " History of Leicester." 4to. 1791.

Throsby's " Select Views of Leicestershire." 2 vols. 4to. 1790.

Transactions of the Leicester Architectural and Archæological Society.

Transactions of the Leicester Literary and Philosophical Society.

Weather-Lore. Richard Inward. London. 1893.

PREFATORY NOTE.

THE classification adopted in this compilation is that
recommended by Mr. G. L. Gomme in "The Handbook
of Folk-Lore," published by the Folk-Lore Society
in 1890, p. 6.

The Editor ventures to suggest that if the same classification be adopted in all forthcoming numbers of this series,
the critical work of reference and comparison will be greatly
facilitated.

It is believed that a large proportion of the *recorded* folk-
lore of the two counties is comprised in the extracts here
given. Many of them may prove to be of no scientific value,
but the Editor thought it wise to be liberal in giving them
the benefit of any possible doubt.

Thanks are due to the Members of the Local Committee
who have assisted the Editor in the task of examining
printed authorities and making extracts, and especially to
those who have begun to collect the oral tradition of the
Counties, a few samples of which are included in these
pages.

Part I.

SUPERSTITIOUS BELIEFS AND PRACTICES.

(a) SUPERSTITIONS CONNECTED WITH INORGANIC NATURAL OBJECTS.

Charley, a spot very near, is called *the Giants' Graves.*   HILLS.
"History and Antiquities of Charnwood Forest."
T. R. Potter, 1842, p. 105.

Bardon.—The recollection that it was one of the high places where the Bards (hence its name) hymned the praises of their Sun-God and their heroes, and where Druidical superstition received its votaries and offered its victims, is one of the many associations connected with Bardon.
"History and Antiquities of Charnwood Forest."
T. R. Potter, 1842, p. 161.
See Nichols, III., 126.

Superstition concerning the Dip of the Rocks.—One venerable old man, at work in the Gate-house quarry, observing me searching for the dip, asked me, with a smile expressive of his consciousness of superior wisdom in such matters, "Which way is Judæa?" I at once pointed my hand in a south-easterly direction. "You are right," replied my mentor; "find Judæa, and you will find the direction of these rocks. Find the dip, and you will point to

Judæa. This is the case over the whole world, and has been so ever since the Saviour's resurrection." I found Professor Sedgwick's anticlinal line theory at once destroyed!!!

Of course I did not attempt to shake a belief that seemed not unmixed with natural piety.

Potter, p. 89.

Beacon Fire.—Mr. Langham, of "Needless Inn," informs me that he well remembers that thirty-four years ago there stood, on the highest point of Beacon, an erection of rude and ancient masonry, about six feet high, of a round form, and having in its centre a cavity about a yard deep and a yard in diameter, the sides of which were very thickly covered with burnt pitch. This, he says, had all the appearance of having been used for holding the beacon fires. He remembers, too, that at that period, the entrenchments above described were much more visible than they are now. He is the only person with whom I have conversed that seems ever to have noticed them, except Mr. William Lester, of Woodhouse; and they are not mentioned by any writer whatever, unless Gale's remark applied to them. I discovered, by digging, many heaps of nearly perished mortar, mingled with fragments of stone and dark red brick.

"History and Antiquities of Charnwood Forest."
T. R. Potter, 1842, p. 48.

Beacon Hill.—Not satisfied with my single opinion of these extraordinary remains, I requested Mr. Lester, a highly intelligent farmer and surveyor, who lives at the foot of Beacon, to examine them. He was perfectly astonished. Though long resident, almost upon the spot, and aware of the remains described as lying on the south-west side of the hill, it had never occurred to him that there were others. "Often," says he, "as I have crossed that wonderful hill, and always with the feeling that it was a *charmed* spot, I have either been so occupied with the distant prospects, or so circumscribed in my immediate view by the inequalities of the surface, that I have never before once noticed the most remarkable fortifications to which you have directed me."

Potter, p. 49.

See also under " Festival Customs." [Wakes.]

Among the hills of Charnwood Forest in Leicestershire are BARROWS. two, the one called Inglebarrow, the other Hiveshead. The former, as may be inferred from the name, was the site of the altar on which sacrifices were offered to the god or gods abiding on the higher Hiveshead. At Humberstone, in the same county, a village owing its name to an *amber* or sacred stone within its boundaries, the *amber*, at which religious rites were performed, was on an eminence in the vicinity of a higher ridge, which, according to the common belief, was the abode of gods.

Dudley's " Naology," p. 189, *note*.

Bagrave.—See Nichols, III., 289.

A ridge of considerable length occurs beside the Roman Foss Road near Ratcliffe-on-Wreke, in the county of Leicester. It is evidently a structure formed, at least in part, by man; and being, like the barrow about a mile distant, near Thurmaston, lately destroyed, situate near a highway anciently of great publicity, it must be regarded as one instance of the long barrow, the true though remote origin of the present form of our churches.

Dudley's " Naology," p. 273, *note*.

King Lud's Entrenchments or *Rents.—See* Nichols, II., 305 ; IV., 1045.

Dr. Stukeley says : " At Cossington, just before I came to the river Wreke, is a vast barrow, 350 feet long, 120 broad, 40 high, or near it. It is very handsomely worked upon the sides, and very steep. . . . They call it *Shipley Hill*, and say a great

BARROWS.   captain, called Shipley, was buried there. I doubt not but this is of great antiquity and Celtic, and that the intent of it is rightly preserved by the country people; but as to the name of him I can say nothing. On the top are several oblong double trenches cut in the turf, where the lads and lasses of the adjacent villages meet upon Easter Monday yearly, to be merry with cakes and ale." * . . . The hill is lately proved to be the wonderful work of nature, not of art, and has been produced by some uncommon surflux of the river Wreke.

Nichols, III., 384.

Robin Hood's Barn.—There is a mound in a flat meadow near the river (at Hoby), part of Earl Ferrers' farm, which the inhabitants (for some unknown reason if there ever was any) call Robin Hood's Barn. It appears to be one of those mounds which the Romans threw up to mark their marches to the rear of their legions.

Nichols, III., 388.

CAVES.   *Black Annis' Bower.*—Every inhabitant of Leicester has been made acquainted with a spot called Black Annis' Bower upon the Dane Hills, near this town, but every one has not been put in possession of the legend as it is embodied in the following lines. They are taken from the Burton MS. (quoted by Nichols), which says they were the production of an " ingenious young poet, whose early loss his friends had much reason to deplore, as a man of superior talents, and his country as a soldier of undaunted courage."

> " Where down the plain the winding pathway falls
> From Glenfield Vill to Lester's ancient walls,
> Nature or Art with imitative power,
> Far in the glenn has placed *Black Annis' Bower.*

---

* An old shepherd still living (1799) remembers these sports, but they have long fallen into disuse.

" An oak, the pride of all the mossy dell,
Spreads its broad arms abcve the stony cell ;
And many a bush, with hostile thorns arrayed,
Forbids the secret cavern to invade ;
Whilst delving vales each way meander round,
And violet banks with redolence abound.

" Here, if the uncouth song of former days
Soil not the page with Falsehood's artful lays,
Black Annis held her solitary reign,
The dread and wonder of the neighbouring plain.
The shepherd grieved to view his waning flock,
And traced his firstlings to the gloomy rock.
No vagrant children culled (the) flow'rets then,
For infant blood oft stained the gory den.

" Not Sparta's mount,* for infant tears renown'd,
Echo'd more frequently the piteous sound.
Oft the gaunt Maid the frantic Mother curs'd,
Whom Britain's wolf with savage nipple nurs'd :
Whom Lester's sons beheld, aghast the scene,
Nor dared to meet the *Monster of the Green.*

" 'Tis said the soul of mortal man recoil'd,
To view Black Annis' eye, so fierce and wild ;
Vast talons, foul with human flesh, there grew
In place of hands, and features livid blue
Glar'd in her visage ; while the obscene waist
Warm skins of human victims close embraced.

" But Time, than Man more certain, tho' more slow,
At length 'gainst Annis drew his sable bow ; †
The great decree the pious shepherds bless'd,
And general joy the general fear confess'd.

" Not without terror they the cave survey,
Where hung the monstrous trophies of her sway :
'Tis said, that in the rock large rooms were found,
Scoop'd with her claws beneath the flinty ground ;
In these the swains her hated body threw,
But left the entrance still to future view,
That children's children might the tale rehearse,
And bards record it in their tuneful verse.

* Mount Taygetus, in a cavern near to which it was the custom to expose deformed and sickly children to perish.

† By poetical license for *scythe.*

1 9

" But in these listless days, the idle bard
Gives to the wind all themes of cold regard ;
Forgive, then, if in rough, unpolished song,
An unskilled swain the dying tale prolong.

" And you, ye Fair, whom Nature's scenes delight,
If Annis' Bower your vagrant steps invite,
Ere the bright sun Aurora's car succeed,
Or dewy evening quench the thirsty mead,
Forbear with chilling censures to refuse
Some gen'rous tribute to the rustic muse.
A violet or common daisy throw,
Such gifts as Maro's lovely nymphs bestow ;
Then shall your Bard * survive the critic's frown,
And in your smiles enjoy his best renown."

To pursue this subject a little further. Burton refers to a gravestone in Swithland Church as follows :—" On a flat grave-stone inlaid with plates of brass, in the body of the chancel (since removed to the present vestry—Ed.), near the entrance into the chancel, is the picture of a woman, veiled : under which is this inscription :

' Hoc in conclave jacet Agnes Scott camerata
Antrix devota Dominae Ferrers Vocitata,
Quiquis eris, qui transieris, quero, funde precata ;
Sum quis eris, fueramque quod es : pro me, precor, ora.'

" In the east window of the chancel is her picture in glass drawn to the life, in the same habit, with a ring on her finger. This *Agnes Scott*, as I guess, was an Anchoress ; and the word *Antrix* in this epitaph coined from *Antrum*, a cave, wherein she lived ; and certainly (as I have been credibly informed) there is a cave near Leicester, upon the west side of the town, at this day called Black Agnes's Bower."

" Leicester Chronicle," Feb. 26th, 1842.

[Repeated in the same newspaper October 24th, 1874. *See* Nichols, III., 1051, *note.* Ed.]

* Lieut. John Heyrick.

About a mile from Leicester, on the west of the town, are low CAVES.
eminences called the Dane Hills, properly the *dunes*, for there is
no reason to suppose that they were ever occupied by the Danes.
The country in that quarter had been in the state of a wild forest
till within a few past centuries. On the side of one of the knolls
of this formerly wild district was a round cave, of diameter of
ten or twelve feet, and height about five, excavated from the
sandstone strata then extant. This cave was known by the name
of *Black Annis's Bower*, said in the country to have been a savage
woman with great teeth and long nails, and that she devoured
human victims. Such were the tales told formerly, but now
almost lost in the darkness of ignorance. The cave, it seems, is
now nearly filled up by soil carried into it by rains, but was,
about seventy years ago, quite open.* The resemblance of this
cave to that seen by Bishop Heber in Bengal is very close and
exact. Were it laid open, it is believed that it would be found
similar to it in every respect—similar also to the cave of the
Black Ceres in Phigalia.

The name of *Annis*, to whom this cave is said to have belonged,
is known to the Celtic mythologist by the name of *Anu* or *Nannu*,
names signifying the mother goddess, according to the authority
of Vallancey, an author well learned in the Celtic language of the
Irish.† He states that she was the same as the British *Ked* or
Ket, and the Grecian Ceres. That she was the same as the Black
Cali of India, and the Black Ceres or Demeter of Greece, is
certain. The ancient Britons, did, no doubt, eat the flesh of the
human victims offered on their altars, as did the Mexicans of later
ages. Consequently the tales of the cannibal practices of Black
Annis of the Bower cannot be without reason doubted, and that
the cannibal rites were often practised near this cavern, most
probably, like the sacrifices at the altar of Trophonius, in the
dead time of night, at a spot hid from ordinary view by the woods

* It may be proper to observe that in this recital the author speaks from
personal experience. He saw it, and was actually in the cave about seventy
years ago.
† Vallancey de Reb. Hibern. c. i., s. 5, p. 490.

CAVES.

and thickets of the then Leicester forest, and attended with circumstances well calculated to horrify any man, but especially the rude and superstitious Britons then present.

Dudley's "Naology," pp. 249-250.

Little children, who went to run on the Dane Hills, were assured that she (Black Anna) lay in wait there, to snatch them away to her "bower"; and that many like themselves she had "scratched to death with her claws, sucked their blood, and hung up their skins to dry."

"Leicester Chronicle," 5th Sep., 1874.

Black Anna was said to be in the habit of crouching among the branches of the old pollard oak (the last remnant of the forest) which grew in the cleft of the rock over the mouth of her cave or "bower", ever ready to spring like a wild beast on any stray children passing below. The cave she was traditionally said to have dug out of the solid rock with her finger nails. On my last visit to the Bower Close, now several years ago, the trunk of the old tree was then standing, but I know not if it still remains. At that time, and long previously, the mouth of the cave was closed, but in my school days it was open, and, with two or three companions, I recollect on one occasion "snatching a fearful joy" by crawling on our hands and knees into the interior, which, as far my recollection serves me at this distance of time, was some seven or eight feet long by about four or five feet wide, and having a ledge of rock, for a seat, running along each side.

F.R.H.S. (William Kelly) in "Leicester Chronicle," 3rd October, 1874.

"I have looked through my deeds . . . . and find that the earliest deeds in my possession, dated 13th and 14th May, 1764, contain the following description:—All that close or parcel of land commonly called or known by the name of 'Black Anny's

Bower Close ' . . . . In the conveyance to myself, the de- CAVES. scription is 'Black Anna's Bower Close.'" . . . .

Letter from the Hon. Sir John Mellor to Editor of "Leicester Chronicle," 7th Nov. 1874.

A relic of this still remains in the minds of people in Leicester in the form of "Cat Anna." Some warehouse girls told me a short time ago that she was a witch who lived in the cellars under the castle, and that there was an underground passage from the cellars to the Dane Hills, along which she ran! *

From Miss Henrietta Ellis.

See also under "Festival Customs" [Easter] and "Place Legends" [Lear].

The Hoston-Stone.—Some years ago I communicated some SACRED remarks, which were inserted in the "History of Leicestershire," STONES. concerning the stone called by the inhabitants of Humberston "Hoston-Stone," or "Hoston;" meaning, perhaps, High-Stone. I have always regarded this stone, though now little noticed, as a very curious object ; and, having made myself of late years better acquainted than when I wrote before with the subjects with which I imagine this stone to be connected, I offer the following remarks, as correcting, in some measure, my former communications.

This stone is one of those blocks of granite found very frequently in the neighbourhood, and supposed by the celebrated De Luc to be fragments cast up by some convulsion of the earth from the primary and deepest strata. The Hoston-Stone lies on the ridge of an eminence, which, though not the highest of the neighbouring hills, is yet very conspicuous for a vast distance from the West. Some old persons in the neighbourhood, still living, remember when it stood a very considerable height, perhaps eight or ten feet, in an artificial fosse or hollow. About fifty or sixty

---

* On December 4th, 1837, a play called "Black Anna's Bower, or the Maniac of the Dane Hills," was performed at the Leicester Theatre. The plot turned upon the celebrated murder of a landlady of the "Blue Boar," related in the Histories of Leicester, and Black Anna played a part similar to that of the Witches in Macbeth. Ed.

years ago the upper parts of the stone were broken off, and the fosse levelled, that a plough might pass over it; but, according to the then frequent remarks of the villagers, the owner of the land who did this deed never prospered afterwards. He certainly was reduced from being the owner of five "yard-land," to use the then common phrase, or about one hundred and twenty acres, to absolute poverty, and died about six years ago in the parish work-house. This superstitious opinion attached to the stone, together with the following circumstances, persuade me to think that the stone was what is usually called "Druidical." It possibly may have been a "logan," or rocking-stone; but of this there certainly is no evidence.

There are, or rather were, about fifty years ago, traditionary tales in the village that a nunnery once stood on Hoston; and that steps had been found communicating subterraneously with the monks of Leicester Abbey, about two miles distant. But no religious house of the kind is to be traced here. The tale must have owed its origin to circumstances connected with the religion of earlier times; probably anterior to the introduction of Christianity into Britain; and therefore during the prevalence of the idolatry of the Britons.

Some years ago it was believed that fairies inhabited, or at least frequented, this stone; and various stories were told concerning those pigmy beings. Such, according to the testimony of Borlase, in his "History of Cornwall," is the common opinion respecting the many Druidical stones in that county. This belief was so strongly attached to the Hoston-Stone, that some years ago a person visiting it alone fancied he heard it utter a deep groan; and he immediately ran away to some labourers, about two hundred yards distant, terrified with the apprehension of seeing one of the wonderful fairy inhabitants.

In the adjoining vale, at the distance of about one hundred yards from the stone, on the north-east, is a plot of ground known, before the inclosure of the lordship, by the name of "Hell-hole Furlong." No circumstance belonging at present to the spot seems likely to have given rise to this strange name: it leaves room, therefore, for the conjecture that in this quarter the sacrifices, too often human, were wont to be performed; and that from this circumstance it obtained the Saxon name of " Hela," or " Death." SACRED STONES.

From these circumstances, and also from the situation of the stone in an eminence, such as were usually chosen for the celebration of the religious rites of the ancient British, there seems to be little room for doubt that Hoston was once sacred to the purposes of Druidical, or rather of the more ancient Bardic, worship. These spots are in some places still termed " Homberds," or " Humberds," probably from the Erse word (according to Vallancey) *uam*, or *owin*, signifying fear, or terror, and *bardh*, the name of a well-known order of priests. The word *humberd*, thus compounded, is but too justly applicable to the scenes of Bardic worship, which were terrible, both from the character of *Dis*, or Pluto, whom they especially worshipped, and from the rites by which he was propitiated.

These conjectures and opinions derive further support from the name of the village within whose liberties this stone is situate. Humberston is very plainly the *ton*, or town, of the *Humberd*, or sacred place of Bardic worship; for the village stands on the south side of the ridge, of which Hoston-height is part, and about half a mile from the stone, which is as near as habitations seem to have been allowed to approach those dreadfully sacred places. The name of Humberston belongs to a village on the coast of Lincolnshire, near Grimsby. Should there be any *Humberd* near it, the conclusion must be, not only that the Lincolnshire village, but the river Humber itself, derived their names from a place of Bardic worship.

Yours, &c., J. D.

" Gentleman's Library Magazine," " English Traditions," p. 123-5, quoting *Gentleman's Magazine*, 1813, part i., pp. 318, 319.

SACRED
STONES.

In the lordship of Humberston, a village near Leicester, on lands belonging to the Pochin family, there is a large erratic block of the syenite rock from the Mountsorrel hills, which, though now covered with soil, was till within a few years past open to view, and was well known to and regarded with a certain degree of awe by many of the inhabitants. It was called the Holy Stone; was said to be attended by fairies; it was believed that any person practising any outrage toward it, or using any indignity, would never prosper. It is believed that this stone was the supporter of an *amber* stone, from which the village obtained the name of Humberston,* or Ambers-ton, the town of the *amber*.† The lands around are known by the name of Hoston, from the stone.

Village traditions idly affirm that there was once a nunnery at this place, and a subterranean passage communicating with Leicester Abbey. This tale probably originated at the Reformation, when every idle assertion tending to render monks odious was greedily swallowed. Not the slightest evidence exists of such structure. The tale, however, is not undeserving attention. It may have been founded on a tradition that a Celtic cave was once extant at the place, perhaps beneath the stone on which the *amber* stood. In the ages of Christianity which followed the suppression of the Celtic religion, it seems to have been designated by the name of Hell Hole. This name is still retained by the lands forming the slope of the eminence on which the Holy stone

---

* There are only two towns in England that bear the name of Humberston; this near Leicester, the other near Grimsby, in the county of Lincoln. Whether there be any *amber* stone near the latter village does not appear, but the singularity of the name leaves little room for doubt that such a stone must once have stood near the place. This Humberston is upon the shore of the estuary called the Humber, which in all probability derived its name from the *amber*, an object perhaps conspicuously placed, which mariners would not fail to reverence as they passed it, according to the known custom of ancient times.

† A low hill in the lordship, of a perfectly round form, crossed by the turnpike road leading to Uppingham, is called *Roborough*, a name evidently compounded of the word barrow and the Celtic *rhóll*, confirming the opinion of the Celtic origin of the village.

is situate, although the richness of the lands and their pleasant aspect seems to demand a less offensive name. These circumstances afford evidence which cannot be reasonably contravened, that the name of Hell Hole was given to a Celtic cave, which, from the tale of the nunnery, may be inferred to have been dedicated to a female divinity, possibly the Black *Annis* of the Leicester cave; and that the odious title was given in reference to the Celtic, possibly the cannibal, sacrifices there performed.

Dudley's "Naology," p. 256.

In June, 1843, I visited the spot, and a ploughman who had worked for many years upon the farm pointed out this Amberstone, or Hoston, to me. It is vulgarly called Hostin. I found it nearly covered with earth and standing corn. The ground around it is slightly conical, arising no doubt from the occasional efforts of the agriculturists to keep it covered. The gradual washing away by the rain of the mound of earth has doubtless given birth to the popular idea of the rising of the stone.

Allies's "Antiquities and Folk-lore of Worcestershire,"
2nd ed., p. 371. *See* pp. 368-371.

The St. John's Stone.—A couple of generations ago there stood in the Abbey Fields, on the north side of the town, a somewhat shapeless stone pillar about seven feet high, called the St. John's Stone. Mr. Thomas Warner, whose farm lies round this stone, tells me that he recollects it in 1835, when its height had been reduced to about three feet, and by 1840 it had been completely destroyed. Fortunately Mr. Flowers' accurate pencil has preserved a representation of it as it appeared in 1817.* All that tradition has handed down to us about the St. John's Stone is contained in Mr. Hollings' paper on "Roman Leicester," † read before this Society, and in Mr. Kelly's latest work, "Royal

---

* This sketch, dated 1815, was in the late Mr. W. Kelly's possession, and was reproduced in his "Royal Progresses," p. 17. Ed.

† Hollings' "Roman Leicester," pp. 15-17. Ed.

Progresses and Visits to Leicester," * and is confined to the state-
ments that it was the custom to visit it on St. John's Day—the
24th of June—and that children who played about it were
careful to leave it before dark because after then the fairies
came and danced round it.

The stone stood in the centre of an amphitheatre—shaped
hollow—just where the hills rise from the level of the valley,
with the horse-shoe of the amphitheatre cutting into the hill-side.
Its floor, upon which the stone must have stood, is a mass of
sand-stone, in which we search in vain for any trace of the hole
or socket, and which, it might have been supposed, would be
necessary to retain, in an upright position, a pillar seven feet
high. . . . .

After giving certain geological details with regard to a neighbouring bed of sand, the writer concludes as follows :—

We have only to suppose that the St. John's Stone was
originally one of the pillars in a similar bed of sand, that the
sand was by some means removed and one of the pillars exposed,
and we should have the St. John's Stone growing, as it were,
from the ground, and not sunk, like an ordinary pillar, into any
hole or socket. Mr. Warner's recollection confirms the foregoing
supposition. He distinctly recollects that the stone was sand-
stone. I cannot help thinking that its rough and unshapely
mass, as it appears in Mr. Flowers' drawing, very fairly answers
to what might have been expected from this method of its forma-
tion. I know no other way of accounting for the presence of such
a block and floor of stone. The grey perishable stone of the
Dane Hills would certainly not satisfy the required conditions.

If our suggested explanation is correct, it at once removes the
St. John's Stone from the class of stones which have been brought
from a distance and set up to mark some spot, such as a battle-
field, or the grave of a king or hero. It belongs rather to the
class of natural but unusual or striking objects which have
always and everywhere excited the imagination of primitive

* P. 697. Ed.

man, and have given rise to the feelings of wonder and awe and SACRED
fear which make up so large a part of his religion. . . . . STONES.

> J. D. Paul, F.G.S., " Leicester Literary and Philo-
> sophical Society Transactions," New Quarterly
> Series, vol. iii., pp. 262-3.

Little John's Stone.—See Nichols, III., 981 and 1054.

Markfield.—This lies on the direct line between Derventio,
Little Chesters, and Ratby, Leicester. At the junction of the
parishes of Markfield and Newtown Linford, as late as 1808,
stood an inscribed stone called the Altar-stone, which has since
disappeared undescribed.

> Evans' " Leicestershire Words," p. 64.

At Markfield, which is also in the direct line from Derventio
to Ratby, there was standing at the time the forest was enclosed
a remarkable stone called "the Altar-Stone." An aged man,
named Jarvis, still living at Markfield, states that he "well
remembers this stone; that it was covered with *outlandish letters*,
and was removed when cultivation began, because it was in the
centre of a field."

> Potter, p. 54.

The fossils called *Astroites* are found in this parish (Lubben-
ham); they are vulgarly called "Peter's Stones." Nichols, II., 700.

Serpentine Stone, amulet of, found at Atherston. Nichols, IV.,
1038, *note*.

The Oaks Hanging Stone.—A spot which is about the centre of
a triangle formed by that stone, Kite Hill, and the Tin Meadows,
was, according to the information of an old forest-keeper of Lord
Hastings', always called "the Grove" before the enclosure. It
may, in early times, have been a grove to some temple, or to the
Hanging Stone Cromlech.

> Potter, p. 44.

SACRED
STONES.

Even in these days the stranger cannot behold the pile without feelings approaching to awe. No one riding up to the lower side of it, on a spirited horse, can fail to observe the emotion of the animal; and an old forester states that Mr. Gisborne's Scotch cattle, on their first arrival, always gaze at it with wonder. " I take care," added he, "never to be near it after twilight has begun."

Ib., p. 43.

See Nichols, III., 134.
See also under " Local Customs." [Swainmote.]

Witch-Stone.—In the Town Museum at Leicester there is a rude, perforated stone, which bears the following label :—

Witch-Stone from Wymeswold.

" This has been preserved for many generations in our family, and till within the last few years great virtues were attributed to it. It prevented the entrance of fairies into the dairy, preserved the milk from taint, kept off diseases, and charmed off warts, etc.

"Presented by T. R. Potter, Esq." (in 1852).*

From Montagu Browne, F.Z.S., Curator.

Mr. T. R. Potter informed me in August, 1852, that in the neighbourhood of Wymeswold more than one perforated stone ring (probably Celtic) is preserved by persons as a charm against witchcraft.

Mr. W. Kelly.

LABY-
RINTHS.

One was some years ago cut out in the smooth turf on a hill in the parish of Liddington, near Uppingham, in the county of Rutland. The hill was called *Priestly Hill*, whence

---

* See Evans's " Ancient Stone Implements of Great Britain," p. 422. (Ed.)

it is inferred that the eminence, which bears the form of a **LABY-** barrow, was once at least regarded as a sacred eminence; and **RINTHS** the act of *running the maze*, the phrase signifying the act of passing over all its windings, was once held to be sacred.

Dudley's "Naology," p. 322, note.

Near the road leading from Medbourn to Holt, about a quarter of a mile from the latter, is a shepherd's race, called here "The Maze."

Nichols, II., 728.

Holy Well Haw.—I gleaned the leading parts of the following **HOLY** Legend of Holy Well from an aged person at Whitwick, where **WELLS.** the name of Comyn, as connected with the ancient castle of that place "a matter of five hundred years ago," is still mentioned.

The popular idea seems to be, that the Comyns were great giants. One of them, said my informant, attempted to carry off one of the ladies of Groby Castle, who left that place for security, intending to take sanctuary at Grace Dieu. Going, however, by a circuitous route, to avoid Charley and Whitwick, she was benighted, and would have perished in the outwoods, but for one of the monks of the Holy Well. The anachronisms and notations of history occurring in the narrative need not be pointed out to the intelligent reader. There is, however, as observed below, some truth mixed up with what is evidently fabulous. The tradition may, in fact, have arisen from Douglas's carrying off Eleanor Ferrars.

Potter, p. 190

LEGEND OF THE HOLY WELL.

> The oaks of the forest were autumn-tinged,
>   And the winds were at sport with their leaves,
> When a maiden traversed the rugged rocks
>   That frown over Woodhouse Eaves.
>
> The rain fell fast—she heeded it not—
>   Though no hut or home appears;
> She scarcely knew if the falling drops
>   Were rain-drops or her tears.

Onward she hied through the outwoods dark—
(And the outwoods were darker then :)
She feared not the forest's deep'ning gloom—
She feared unholy men.

Lord Comyn's scouts were in close pursuit,
For Lord Comyn the maid had seen,
And had marked her mother's only child
For his paramour, I ween.

A whistle, a whoop, from the Buyk Hylls' side
Told Agnes her foes were nigh :
And, screened by the cleft of an aged oak
She heard quick steps pass by.

Dark and dread fell that autumn night :
The wind-gusts fitful blew :
The thunder rattled ; the lightning's glare
Showed Beacon's crags to view.

The thunder neared—the light'ning played
Around that sheltering oak ;
But Agnes, of men, not God afraid,
Shrank not at the light'ning's stroke !

The thunder passed—the silvery moon
Burst forth from her cave of cloud,
And showed in the glen " red Comyn's " men,
And she breathed a prayer aloud :—

" Maiden mother of God ! look down—
List to a maiden's prayer :
Keep undefiled my mother's sole child—
The spotless are thy care."

    *   *   *   *

The sun had not glinted on Beacon Hill
Ere the Hermit of Holy Well
Went forth to pray, as his wont each day,
At the Cross in Fayre-oke dell.

Ten steps had he gone from the green grassy mound
Still hemming the Holy Well Haw,
When, stretched on the grass—by the path he must pass—
A statue-like form he saw !

He crossed himself once, he crossed himself twice,
   And he knelt by the corse in prayer ;
" Jesu Maria ! cold as ice—
   Cold—cold—but still how fair ! "

The Hermit upraised the stiffened form,
   And he bore to the Holy Well ;
Three Paters or more he muttered o'er,
   And he filled his scallop shell.

He sprinkled the lymph on the maiden's face,
   And he knelt and he prayed at her side—
Not a minute's space had he gazed on her face
   Ere signs of life he spied.

      •   •   •   •

Spring had invested the Charnwood oaks
   With their robe of glist'ning green,
When on palfreys borne one smiling morn
   At the Holy Well Haw were seen

A youth and a lady, passing fair,
   Who asked for the scallop shell :
A sparkling draft each freely quaffed,
   And they blessed the Holy Well.

They blessed that Well, and they fervently blessed
   The holy Hermit too ;
To that and to him they filled to the brim
   The scallop, and drank anew.

" Thanks, Father ! Thanks !—To this Well and thee,"
   Said the youth, " but to Heav'n most,
I owe the life of the fairest wife
   That Charnwood's bounds can boast.

" The blushing bride thou seest at my side
   (Three hours ago made mine)
Is she who from death was restored to breath
   By Heav'n's own hand and thine.

" The Prior of Ulverscroft made us one,
   And we hastened here to tell
How much we owe kind Heav'n and thee
   For the gift of the Holy Well.

"In proof of which—to the Holy Well Haw
   I give, as a votive gift,
From year to year three fallow deer,
   And the right of the Challenge drift.

"I give, besides, of land two hides,
   To be marked from the Breedon Brand ;
To be held while men draw from the Well in this Haw
   A draught with the hollow hand."

The Hermit knelt, and the Hermit rose,
   And breathed " Benedicite "—
" And tell me," he said, with a hand on each head
   " What Heav'n-sent pair I see ? "

" This is the lost De Ferrars' child
   Who dwelt at the Steward's Hay ;
And, father, my name— yet unknown to fame—
   Is simply Edward Grey."

Potter, p. 191.
[*See* Nichols, III., 122. Ed.]

St. James's Well.—It may be well to mention that in close proximity to the Chapel of St. Sepulchre stood St. James's Chapel, which had a holy well in connection with it, close to the old pond at the corner of Infirmary Square. This well had a never-failing supply of fresh water, until the deep drainage of the town diverted it from its original outlet.

William Kelly. " Leicestershire Notes and Queries,"
vol. ii., p. 82.
See " Notes and Queries," "Choice Notes," p. 205. Ed.

Hinckley.—St. Mary's, or Our Lady's Well.

There is a well here known as St. Mary's Well, or more commonly as Our Lady's Well; it still supplies most excellent water to all the neighbourhood.

Hope. " Holy Wells," p. 87.

In Sketchley, a hamlet in Burbage parish, near Hinckley, there is a well, now enclosed, which once had the reputation of brightening rustic brains. A quick repartee or smart saying was sure to be greeted, "Oh, you've been to Sketchley lately"; or a dullard would be recommended to "go to Sketchley."

"Leicester Chronicle," 8th June, 1874.

Ratby.—At Ratby, four miles north-west of Leicester, is a place called the Holy Well; the waters are anti-scorbutic.

Other holy wells are St. Austin's in Leicester (the water from which well was formerly in great repute as a remedy for sore eyes), Holywell Haw, and those at Ryhall dedicated to St. Tibba and St. Eabba.

"Holy Wells; their Legends and Superstitions,"
by R. C. Hope, F.S.A., F.R.S.A., pp. 86-87,
127-128.
"Leicestershire N. and Q.," iii., p. 72.
Nichols, I., 301, 434.

St Tibba's Well, Rutland.—Ryhall: St. Tibba's Well, and St. Eabba's, or Jacob's Well.—There was here a well and a shrine in honour of St. Tibba. "'Tis now above 700 years since St. Tibba, the celebrated saint of Ryhall, was taken out of her grave there and carried to Peterborough Church by Abbot Elgin. The inhabitants there have still an obscure memorial of her, but lost her name. They call her Queen, and say she used to walk up to Tibbal's Hill, and wash her in a spring there. This is all they know of her. The truth is, on Tibbal's Hill is the spring which gave name to the hill, Tibb's-Well-Hill. 'Tis upon the hill going from Tolethorp to Belinsford Bridge. On the brow of the hill near the spring is Halegreen, as it is still called, taking its name from the anniversary meetings held in former times, in memory of St. Tibba, whose day is December 16th. Hale is the name our Saxon ancestors gave to the solemnities they practised in the fields to the honour of the saints. St. Tibba's Well is now corrupted into Stibbal's-Hill-Well."

"Just above Ryhall is Stablesford Bridge, which, being an odd name upon the River Guash, this opinion is proposed about it. When we read of St. Tibba, we find St. Eabba, her cousin, along with her, another devout, retired person, who commonly lived with her. Hence I conjecture that the spring just above this bridge, northward on the brow of the hill, as it were, opposite to St. Tibba's Well, was consecrated by our pious ancestors to St. Eabba. Then this ford over the river, before the bridge was built, would be called St. Eabba's-Well-Ford, corrupted into Stablesford. This same spring is now called by the shepherds Jacob's Well, and that probably is but a corruption of St. Eabba's Well.

Saints Tibba and Eabba were of royal Mercian blood, and owned Ryhall. They were at first wild hunting girls, at last Saints."

> Stukeley's " Diaries and Letters," iii., 167-70 (Surtees Soc., vol. lxxx.), quoted in " Leicestershire N. and Q.," ii., 208 and 259, and " Hope's Holy Wells," pp. 127-128.
>
> *See also* " Festival Customs." [St. Tibba's Day.]

Pin-well or *Pinnals*, in Merevale.

Holwell, Holewells, Holy-Well, &c. Names of Leicestershire Wells.   Evans, p. 84.

In excavating for sewerage purposes in Church Gate, Leicester, in 1853 or 1854, near the south-west corner of Burley's Lane, a very large quantity of *pins* were discovered in the site of what had evidently been an ancient spring or watercourse.

> From Mr. W. Kelly.

Holwell Mouth, the source of a considerable brook in the Vale of Belvoir. . . . The *Fountain Head* is constantly kept in decent repair. . . . There is a large and commodious arbour adjoining the spring, with seats all round it within, and a stone table in the middle.

> Nichols, II., p. *20.

The spring called *Haliwell* near Croxton Abbey.

Nichols, II., p. 151.

> *See also* Nichols, ii., 269 (Burton Lazars); ii., 308
> (Hol-well Spring in the Manor of Bescaby);
> ii., 15 (Holwell, Holy-well, near Ab Kettleby);
> i., 591 (Well by S. Martin's Church, Leicester);
> i., 558 (Well under the tower of S. Margaret's
> Church, Leicester); iv., 130 (Chapel Well,
> Claybrook); iv., 257 (St. John's Well, Lough-
> borough); iv., 335 (Shawell, Sawelle, Shatte-
> well, Shachewell, Shaddeswell, Stachewell,
> Schadwell, or Stathewell); iv., 705 (Holy
> Well, Hinckley); iv., 863 (Pin Well); iv., 897
> (Golden Well, Sapcote); ii., 510 (Our Lady's
> Well, Bradley); ii., 708 (Papillon); iii., 615
> (Holy Well, near Ashby-de-la-Zouch); iii., 840
> (Monk's Well, near Garendon). Ed.

Breedon.—A dove legend, Mr. Jones declares,[*] is attached to **BUILDINGS.**
Breedon Church in Leicestershire, which stands alone on the top
of a high hill, with the village at its foot. They began building
it within the village; but the site was changed, because, it was
said, every night the stones laid during the day were carried up
to the hill-top by doves.

> "Folk-Lore and Provincial Names of British Birds,"
> by the Rev. C. Swainson (Folk-Lore Society),
> 1886, p. 170.
> [See also "Notes and Queries," v., 436; "Choice
> Notes" (Folk-Lore), p. 1; and cf. Gomme
> "Folk-Lore Relics of Early Village Life."
> London, 1883, p. 43, where parallel instances
> are given.—Ed.]

---

[*] The allusion appears to be to "Credulities Past and Present," by W. Jones,
F.S.A., London, 1880.

BUILDINGS.   *Kibworth Church.*—Tradition affirms that the church was intended to be built, and the building actually commenced, about two miles from the village, and near to the Debdale "side-gate," in a field now called Churchyard Close; but that the stones laid in the daytime were removed by supernatural agency during the night to the spot where the present edifice stands. This state of things continued for some time, until the would-be builders at length despairing of ever being able to erect a structure on the site fixed upon, decided to commence building on the spot chosen by the spirits, where the work was accordingly commenced, and proceeded uninterruptedly, until the sanctuary was completed.

"Leicester Chronicle," 27th Feb., 1875.

Smithy, sb. *a smith's shop*: often used as a familiar word for dwelling-house or home.

"Ah'm still at th' o'd smithy."

Evans, p. 244.

SUBTER-   Mr. Carte (Carte's MS. British Museum) mentions a tradition
RANEAN   respecting a vaulted passage from the Castle (at Groby) to
PASSAGES.   Bradgate.   There is another respecting a similar subterranean communication with Leicester, and the villagers of Newtown Linford still give credence to the tradition of another with Ulverscroft Priory.   "In these," adds Mr. Bloxham, "I can find no foundation except in that love of the marvellous, so common in Roman Catholic times, and so peculiar to the lower classes of this kingdom."

"History and Antiquities of Charnwood Forest," T. R. Potter, 1842, p. 113.

See also under "Sacred Stones" [Hoston-Stone], and "Caves" [Black Annis' Bower],

See also Nichols, III., 274; IV., 632.

Need-fires.—I can remember in my youthful days one occasion **FIRE.** when the farmers drove their cattle through the smoke made by need-fires in a time of cattle plague.

Holmes, p. 50.

> *See also* under "Festival Customs" [Easter Eve, Holy Fire, All Saints' Day], "Local "Customs," and "Funeral Customs."

(*b*) TREE AND PLANT SUPERSTITIONS.

Copt Oak, a trysting tree of the olden time, stands on the high **OAKS.** grounds on the west (of Ulverscroft). On this spot (it may have been under this tree) Erick the Forester is said to have harangued his forces against the Norman invaders. It was long a place of assembly on matters connected with the forest, or perhaps a swainmote court.

Potter, p. 150.

Copt Oak.—On an eminence not far distant from the high hills of Bardon, and nearly in the centre of Charnwood Forest, in the county of Leicester, grows an aged oak, called the Copt Oak, which, from several extraordinary circumstances, may be believed to have been an object held sacred by the British Druids, and to have really been a Celtic idol called a *Tau*. Such idols were formed, as above stated, by cutting away the branches of a gigantic oak, and affixing a beam, forming a cross with the bare trunk. The epithet copt, or copped, may be derived from the Celtic *cop*, a head, and evidently indicated that the tree had been *headed* and reduced to the state of a bare trunk. That it was gigantic when entire is evident from an actual measurement in its present state. The remains of the trunk, which is twenty feet high, the height proper for the *Tau*, show that the circumference at the ground was, or rather is (for by boring the earth an accurate measure-

ment has been made), twenty-four feet; at the height of ten feet
the girth is twenty, giving a diameter of near seven feet, or more
than two yards.

If the tree ever formed a Celtic *Tau*, it must be more than two
thousand years old. The present state suggests the idea that this
is very possible. This vast tree is now reduced to a mere shell,
between two and three inches only in thickness, being about two-
thirds of the original circumference, perforated by several
openings, and alive only in about one-fourth of the shell, bearing
small branches, but such as could not have grown when the tree
was entire: then it must have had branches of a size not less than
an oak of ordinary dimensions. This is evident from one of the
openings in the upper part of the shell of the trunk, exactly such
as a decayed branch would produce. These remains stand just
within the bounding wall of the area or consecrated yard of the
chapel newly built, and called the Copt Oak Chapel. There is no
surrounding wall or fence, nor are there any appearances of such
an inclosure. It is very probable that when first consecrated it
was surrounded by an open glade in a grove, which constituted a
Celtic temple; such grove has, however, been felled, yet the
Copt Oak has been spared, but it stands in the vicinity of a wood,
once part of the supposed grove, and not one hundred yards
distant.

The ancient and long-continued celebrity of the Copt Oak
accords with the opinion of its former sacredness. It was, before
the inclosure, as writes the animated and accurate Potter, the
historian of the forest of Charnwood, one of the three places at
which *Swainmotes* were held, always in the open air, for the
regulation of rights and claims on the forest; and persons have
been known even in late times to have attended such motes.
The active-minded historian above-named observes, " At this spot,
it may be under this tree, Edric the forester is said to have
harangued his forces against the Norman invasion; and here too,
in the Parliamentary troubles of 1642, the Earl of Stamford
assembled the trained bands of the district." These facts mark

the Copt Oak extraordinary, and show, that notwithstanding the OAKS. lapse of two thousand years, the trunk was at that distant period a sacred structure, a Celtic idol; and that it is illustrative of antiquarian records.

Dudley's "Naology," pp. 136-138.

The three courts of the forest of Charnwood met in the open air; that of the lordship of Whitwick, near Sharpley Rocks, where the place may still be traced. It is called the Swainmote Rock, and below it is a spot bearing the name of Lady Aspin's Pool, a legend of which is printed in Potter's "History and Antiquities of Charnwood Forest" (p. 156).* The court of the lordship of Groby met at Copt Oak, which stands on high ground, and derives its name from the fact of once having been surrounded with a coped wall (*Ibid.*, 150.) † And the court of the lordship of Sheepshed met on Iveshead, one of the most important of the forest hills. It is isolated from the general range, and from one view presents a bold outline, with a double summit like a saddleback. Swain's Hill, the spot where the swainmote court met, lies at the foot of Iveshead, and a little distance from it stands the "Hangman's Stone," which furnishes the subject of a ballad legend. (*Ibid.*, p. 177.)

G. L. Gomme, "Primitive Folk-Moots," 1880, p. 137.

Two Copt Oaks figure in the local nomenclature.

Evans, p. 129.
[See also Nichols, III., 1094. Ed.]

The age of Copt or Kopft (German : Kopfen, to pollard, behead) Oak, near Ulverscroft, is unknown.

Kirby, "Leicestershire Flora," p. 130.

Holyoke, or *Holy Oaks.* Nichols, II., 607.

---

* *See also* Nichols, III., 134. Ed.

† [" *Cop:* to strike on the head, to decapitate ; to pollard." Evans's " Leicestershire Glossary," p. 129. Ed.]

OAKS.

May 29th, Royal Oak Day.—The children of Leicestershire make this their·May Day, when they go about from house to house with sticks stuck about with flowers and streamers among any available greenery of the season.   They recite this rhyme :—

> " A stig and a stag,
> And a very fine flag
> And a Maypole."

Northall, " Folk Rhymes," p. 244, quoting Evans, p. 255.   Ed.

When they come round begging for a bonfire on November 5th, the formula restores the word to its more usually accepted pronunciation :—

> " A stick and a stake
> For King James's sake,
> And a bonfire, O ! "

Evans, *loc. cit.*

See also under " Festival Customs " [Maypoles, 29th May].

Tree Decay.—Driving round Charnwood Forest, Leicestershire, in the spring of 1893, I was told by my driver, hired from Lough-borough, that the old oaks were said to have *lost their tops* when Lady Jane Grey, who resided at Bradgates * Hall in that neigh-bourhood, was beheaded !   A curious argument from analogy.

G. H. Skipworth in " Folk-Lore," vol. v., p. 169.

GARTREE
BUSH.

In the lordship of Shankton, not quite three-quarters of a mile north of the town, is *Gartree Bush*, famous for having formerly the Hundred Court kept upon the spot.

Nichols II., 781.

[*See* " Leicestershire N. and Q." iii., p. 165.   Ed.]

Stanywells.—At the north-west corner of a wood called Stany-wells are the remains of a tree, which within these few years by

* Bradgate.   Ed.

some accident has been destroyed, round which a regular mound .STANY-
and trench are discernible; where, it is thought, the manor courts WELLS.
for this liberty (Ulverscroft) used formerly to be holden.

Nichols, III., 1094.

See also Potter, 150.

By a cruel superstition shrew mice were formerly entombed ASH TREES.
alive in these trees, to afford a charm against sickness in cattle.
Another custom scarcely less revolting was to pass injured
children through the young stem of an ash split for that purpose.

Kirby, p. 94.

See also under "Leechcraft."

Mapplewell.—The earliest name of this hamlet, Mapulwell MAYPOLES.
(May-pole-well), inclines me to think that on this spot the Druids
were accustomed to celebrate the Bel-Tein,* and, subsequently,
the ancient foresters to offer honours to Flora. The author of
"The Way to Things by Words, and by Words to Things," has
some observations on these rural sacrifices that render such a
supposition not an unnatural one. He says: "The Column of the
May (whence our Maypole) was the great standard of justice in
the Ey-Commons, or Fields of May. Here it was that the people,
if they saw cause, deposed or punished their governors, their
barons, or their kings. The judges' bough or wand (at this time
discontinued, or faintly represented by a nosegay) and the staff or
rod of authority, the mace, as well as the term 'mayor,' were all
derived from this. The youths and maidens joined on these
occasions in singing songs, of which the chorus was, 'We have
brought the summer home.'"†

Potter, p. 93.

Knossington.—In the town street stands a tapered column

---

* This festival may still be traced in the mountains of Cumberland and on
the Cheviot Hills. Mr. Pennant, in his "Tour in Scotland," gives a particular
description of it.

† Ency. Londin. Article "May."

MAYPOLES. called a Maypole, consisting of several cylindrical pieces of oak joined one upon another with dogs and cramps of Iron.

Nichols, II., 657.

See also under " Festival Customs " [Mayday].

FLORAL
RENTS.

Pertaining to the Manor of Groby.—A rent of assize of the Forest of Charnwood of new grubbed-up ground, of £7 6s. 4d.; a rent of hens of the said forest, 9s.; five pounds of pepper, nine pounds of cummin seed, five pairs of gloves, one ounce of silk, one dozen of knots of Kalcedon, six dozen of iron arrows, one clove gillyflower, worth yearly, 7s. 7d.

Potter, p. 107.

Floral Rents in Leicestershire and Rutland.—Nichols[*] tells us that, in 1608, Adrian Farnham, Esq., held freely certain lands and tenements in Woodhouse called Rusha Fields, and other lands there, paying yearly on Midsummer Day one red rose garland and a broad arrow-head with two rosebuds and suit of court at Beaumanor. At the commencement of the present century " the garland, spear, and rosebuds " were regularly sent, and were always placed, according to usage, on the curious chair just described.[†] The garland of flowers now always to be seen thereon is the representative of this ancient chief rent. It is sent in the autumn of each year to Beaumanor, from Mr. Farnham, the owner of Rusha Fields, in the parish of Woodhouse, to the owner of Beaumanor, as, I presume, the lord of the manor of Woodhouse. Under what tenure the fields are held I cannot say, for although the floral chief rent is regularly sent, the owner of Rusha Fields has never, in living recollection, attended the court of the lord of the manor. This garland—which it is now said must contain three roses—is always hung upon the before-mentioned large chair in the hall at Beaumanor, and there it remains until replaced by the fresh garland of the succeeding year. A floral chief

* " Hist. Leicest.," vol. iii., p. 146.
† *Ibid.,* p. 147.

rent is by no means an uncommon acknowledgment. The manor FLORAL
of Stretton, Rutland, was held by the Seagraves of the Crown by the RENTS.
service of one clove gilliflower; and a similar rent was reserved
in a grant made in this year 1274 by John de Burgh, of the
manor of Elmore, Gloucestershire, to Andrew de Gyse. A rose,
however, was the more common service. Walter de Cambron
granted lands, &c., in Leighton to Newminster Abbey for the rent
of one rose on the feast of St. James; Lionel, Earl of Ulster,
granted the Bailiffry of Cork to Geoffrey Stukeley by tenure of a
rose to be paid on St. John the Baptist Day.* Numberless other
instances might be quoted, but it will suffice to quote one more,
and that an example close at hand. By a deed of lease, dated
in 1636, and preserved in the muniment-room of the Corporation
of Leicester, we learn that a piece of ground was sold in fee farm
to James Seele and Elizabeth his wife, who were to have the
same "To be holden of our said soveraigne lord the King his heirs
and successors as of his honour of Leicester in the right of his
Highnes' Dutchy of Lancaster by fealtye only in ffree and comon
soccage, and not in capite: Yielding and paying therefor yearlye
unto the Maior of the Burrough of Leicester for the time being
one damask rose at or upon the feast day of Saint John the
Baptist, and also Yielding and Paying all chief rents yearlye
yssueing or goinge forth of the same." The payment of this floral
rent is noticed occasionally in the Chamberlains' Accounts; for
instance, under date of 1673-4, I find :

"In Loseby Lane :
"Item of him (John Underwood) more for a
piece of ground paying yearly att Midsummer
a damask rose .   .   .   .   .   .   a damask rose."

And in 1677-8 the heirs of Widow Harlow paid the same. The
rent is still receivable, and is paid to the Corporation by the
owner of the "Crown and Thistle" Inn in Loseby Lane, a receipt

* "Notes and Queries," 5th S., ix., 497, and x., 115 and 157.

being annually given to the present esteemed proprietor, Mrs.
Julia Lee, for the damask rose.*

It may be added that sometimes the easy service of a rose was
clogged with curious conditions; in one instance, in a grant made
in the year 1352, it was required that a white rose be rendered
before sunrise at the west end of a particular toft on St. John
Baptist's Day.†

> Thomas North, F.S.A., "Leicestershire N. and Q.,"
> i., pp. 219, 220.   Potter, p. 85.

> [Cf. Grimm, "Teutonic Mythology" (Stalybrass), i.,
> p. 58, and elsewhere.   Ed.]

Floral Rent.—"John Wemerham, of Haverburgh, gives, grants,
and confirms to John Pyfford, of the same, a curtilage situated
between the tenement lately Robert Michell's on the south, and a
messuage of the said John Pyfford's on the north, and abutting on
[   ] of Dag Lane in Haverburgh, to have and to hold, &c.,
at the yearly rent of one flower, payable on the Feast of the
Nativity of Saint [   ], for all secular services.—3 Edward
IV. die Veneris proxima post (festum) Pasche, *i.e.*, Friday, April
15th, 1463."

> Stocks' "Market Harborough Parish Records," p. 177.

Scattering Hemp Seed.—If a young girl went round the churchyard on Midsummer Eve, at midnight, scattering hemp seed, as
the clock struck twelve, and repeating these words—

> " Hemp seed, hemp seed, here I sow,
> Let my true love come after me and mow,"

if she were to be married she would hear her future husband
reaping behind her.

A lady, seventy-two, states that her grandmother had told her

---

* It is not now paid (1894).   Ed.
† "Notes and Queries," 5th S., x., 16.

that she (the grandmother) had scattered hemp seed in the HEMP
churchyard when she was a girl on Midsummer Eve and that she SEED.
could feel her lover's scythe so close to her heels that she was
afraid her feet would be cut off.

From Miss S. A. Squires.   (See Northall, p. 180.   Ed.)

Buttercups.—Children hold buttercups under each other's chins PLANTS.
to see if they love butter.

Kirby, " Leicestershire Flora," p. 4.

Milk-wort has the reputation of curing snake-bites.

Kirby, p. 16.

Wild Teasel (Dipsacus Sylvestris), also called " Venus's bath,"
the water held in the hollows of the leaves being esteemed a
cosmetic, also good for diseases of the eyes.

Kirby, p. 78.

Vipers' Bugloss (Echium vulgare).—The seed resembles a
serpent's head : the plant is reputed not only an antidote to the
bite, but it is said that, carried in the hand, it will keep vipers
at a distance.

Kirby, p. 112.

Ferns.—The burning of ferne doth bring down raine.   (Quoted
in a letter from Belvoir, 1636.)

Nichols, II., 418.

See also under " Leechcraft," " Superstitions," and
" Traditional Customs."

(c) ANIMAL SUPERSTITIONS.

BEES.

Bees.—" Telling the Bees " in Rutland.—An instance of carrying out the well-known superstition concerning bees occurred recently at a hamlet named Geeston, in the parish of Ketton, Rutland. After the death of an old bee-keeper his widow knocked at several bee-hives and said, " He's gone! He's gone! " The bees hummed in reply, by which it is understood that they will remain.

N. Edis, " Leicestershire N. and Q.," i., p. 137.

A death in the family should always be officially notified to the bees, who will resent the slight cast upon them, as members of the household, by the non-performance of the ceremony, by forsaking the hive or dying. I have endeavoured in vain to ascertain the formula, if any, appropriate to the occasion. The melancholy intelligence, however, is certainly sometimes, and I believe always, conveyed in a whisper.

Evans, p. 102.

A piece of crape must always be put on hives when there is a death in the family, or the bees will not thrive.

Also any great piece of news concerning the family must be told them.

From Mrs. J. D. Paul.

To *tang* bees is to make " rough music " with a bell, warming-pan, shovel, or some such instrument when a hive is swarming, for the double purpose, it is said, of asserting a claim to the ownership of the swarm and of collecting the bees together.

Evans, p. 268.

See also under " Proverbs."

Wren and Robin.—*Jenny and Jenny Wren: the wren Motacilla* BIRDS *troglodytes.*—It is thought sacrilegious to kill a robin or a wren, and even to take their eggs is a profanity certain to bring ill-luck, because—

> " The robin and the Jenny Wren
> Are God Almighty's cock and hen."

Evans, p. 178.

It is considered very unlucky if a robin enters a house. He must be prevented from crossing the threshold.

From a Leicestershire domestic servant.

Magpie.—On seeing a magpie it is customary to make the sign of the cross on the ground with the foot.

From a native of Langton.

Crows.—It is unlucky for one crow to fly across your path.

From a native of Woodhouse Eaves.

(Cf. Ælian, " De Nat. Animalium," iii., 9. Ed.)

The rhyme is—

> " One for sorrow, two for mirth,
> Three for a wedding, four for a birth."

If a *cock* comes near to the window or door and crows, a visitor will presently arrive at the house.

From a native of Woodville, near Ashby-de-la-Zouch.

The Green Wood-Pecker—*Picus viridis* (L)—is called the Rain-bird.

Evans, p. 222.

[Cf. Aubrey, " Remaines of Gentilisme," Folk-Lore Society, 1880, p. 258. Ed.]

BIRDS.

Merry-thought of a Fowl.—Is called the "Wishing Bone."

Evans, p. 291.

It is pulled for luck.

[Cf. Aubrey, op. cit., p. 92.   Ed.]

The Breast-bone of a Fowl.—Two single people place the thumbs of their right hands on either side of the flat part that projects from the arch of the bone, and break the bone, one then takes the two pieces and partially conceals them in her hand, the other draws; whichever has the shorter bone will be the first to marry.

From a native of Woodhouse.

A belief in *the Seven Whistlers*, and the ill-luck attendant on their being heard, is universal, but what the Seven Whistlers may be I never could learn, though I have made pertinacious inquiry. More than once I have been told that the "develin," the common swift, is one of them, but I could elicit no further information. I have, however, a thousand times in a summer heard the noise which is said to be made by the Seven Whistlers. It is simply the well-known "scream," as White of Selborne calls it, of the swift, which is loudest and most frequent in thundery weather, and is often heard when the birds themselves are out of sight. The belief in the Seven Whistlers seems to be as common on the continent as in England, and is apparently universal in the Spanish peninsula, but the accepted explanation of the peculiar whistle there heard is that it proceeds from a flight of wild ducks.

Evans, p. 235.

The Leicestershire colliers also believe that the cry of the Seven Whistlers (Golden Plovers) warn them of some calamity, and, on hearing it, refuse to descend into the pit till next day.

Swainson's "Folk-lore of British Birds," p. 181.

It is almost universally believed by the colliers that when any BIRDS.
person will shortly be killed at the pits strange mysterious sounds
are heard in the air at night, sometimes like the distant singing
of a flock of birds, and at other times resembling the smothered
wailings of children chanting a funeral dirge. These they take
to be warnings of the coming calamity, and frequently when
certain unexplainable sounds have been heard at night some of
the men could not be persuaded to go to work on the following
day. Their method of accounting for this strange story is that
seven colliers were once intoxicated on a Sunday, and towards
night they proposed to whistle for a wager to pay for some more
drink, when, fearful to relate, they were all carried up into the clouds
by a whirlwind from which they have never been able to descend,
but, at the return of darkness, their fearful employment is to fly
from place to place, when fatal accidents are impending, to warn,
in premonitory strains of dismal melody, their survivors to avoid
their own terrific and never-dying destiny as "The Seven
Whistlers."

It seems more than probable that the "Seven Whistlers" had
a more ancient origin than in the days of our puritanical fore-
fathers, when the view concerning the Sabbath suggested in the
account first became general. It is more likely that the superstition arose in ancient heathen times among the Teutonic tribes
settled in ancient Germany, from whom the inhabitants of
Worcestershire, descended from a thoroughly Saxon ancestry, may
have received the story.

"Leicester Chronicle," Feb. 12th, 1853.

On Friday, the 16th inst., a collier was making holiday in this
town, and was asked by a tradesman in the market-place why
he was not at his usual work. The reply he made was that none
of the men had gone to work that day because they had heard
the "Seven Whistlers," which he said were birds sent by
Providence to warn them of an impending danger, and that when
they heard that signal not a man would go down he pit until

BIRDS.

the following day. Upon the tradesman suggesting that the collier's account might all be traced to superstition, the poor collier was offended to find his story called in question, and assured the tradesman that the warning was always to be depended upon, for on the two occasions previous to last Friday, when the Seven Whistlers were heard, some colliers foolishly descended the pit, and two lives were lost on each occasion.

"Leicester Chronicle," 24th March, 1855.

See " Allies' Antiquities and Folk-lore of Worcestershire " (2nd edition), p. 459, where it is stated
that the legend has been noticed in the
" Athenæum " (for Sept. 19th and Nov. 14th,
1846, pp. 995, 1162, 1163) in connection with a
curious account in Grimm's " German Mytho-
logy," descriptive of the "Swan Maidens," who
are represented as being heard flying through
the air at night. *See also* Appendix to the
same work (p. 5), where the legend is shown
current in Hertfordshire. *See also* Henderson's
" Folk-lore of Northern Counties," p. 131. The
superstition is referred to by Spenser in the
" Faerie Queen," by Scott in the " Lady of the
Lake " [" The Signal Whistlers "], and more
than once by Wordsworth [" The Seven Birds
that never part," &c.].

See also *Gentleman's Magazine,* 1856, pt. i., pp.
38 - 40. " Gentleman's Magazine Library,"
Popular Superstitions, p. 135. Also see
Leland's " English Gipsies and their language,"
2nd ed., 1874, p. 218, where the gipsy story of
the " Seven Whistlers " is given. The author
refers to a similar superstition in Lord Lytton's
" Harold." Ed.

Eggs Unlucky.—There are many farmers' wives, even in the EGGS. present day, who would never dream of allowing eggs to be brought into the house, or taken out of it, after dark, this being deemed extremely unlucky. "Cuthbert Bede" mentions the case of a famer's wife in Rutland who received a setting of ducks' eggs from a neighbour at nine o'clock at night. "I cannot imagine how she could have been so foolish," said the good woman, much distressed; and her visitor, upon inquiry, was told that ducks' eggs brought into a house after sunset would never be hatched.

> C. G. Leland, "Gypsy Sorcery and Fortune Telling."
> Quoted in "Leicestershire Notes and Queries,"
> vol. ii., p. 2.

Hat Bat.—The bloody bat, *Vespertilio noctula;* the largest BATS. English specimen.

> Evans, p. 168

Village children sing when they see a bat—

> " Hat-bat, come under my hat,
> And I'll give you a piece of bacon."

From Mrs. Bernard Ellis. (See Northall, 324. Ed.

Cats suck the breath of children and so kill them. CATS.

> From Mrs. J. D. Paul.

If the first lamb you see in the spring faces you, you will LAMBS. have good luck for the remainder of the year.

> From a native of Woodhouse.

If you turn your money in your pocket when you see the first lamb of the season, you will have money in your purse for the rest of the year.

> From the same.

PIGS.

It is unlucky to kill a pig in the wane of the moon; if it is done, the pork will shrink in boiling.

From Mrs. J. D. Paul.

See also under " Leechcraft." [Charm against Drunkenness.]

DEVIL'S COACH-HORSE.

Zoerius oleus Ocypus oleus (L)—This unprepossesing insect is considered an harbinger of ill-luck.

Evans, p. 137.

SHEEP.

Sheep.—I have heard of a *bone* taken from a *sheep's skull* being kept in the pocket to keep away disease, but I do not know the name of the bone nor of the disease.

From Miss S. A. Squires.

HORSES.

White Horse.—To meet a white horse without spitting at it (spitting averts all evil consequences) is considered very unlucky in the Midland counties.

Black, " Folk Medicine," p. 117.

ADDERS.

Adder-skin.—" It'll bring you good luck to hang an ether-skin o'er the chimbly "   Heard in Leicestershire.

" Notes and Queries," vii., p. 152. " Choice Notes " (Folk-Lore), p. 243.

For Vipers and Serpents *see* under " Tree and Plant Superstitions."

DOG.

The howling of a dog at night under the window of a sickroom is looked upon as a warning of death's being near.

From Mrs. J. D. Paul.

For Spiders, Mice, Snails, Cows, *see* under " Superstitions."

For Cocks, Cats, Hares, Bulls, Sheep, *see* under " Festival Customs."

For Cats *see also* under " Caves " and " Witchcraft."

For Snails *see also* under " Games."

For Doves *see* under " Buildings."

(*d*) **GOBLINDOM.**

Buried people are believed to walk as ghosts, or " come again " GHOSTS. as the phrase is.

" Maaster! Maaster! Theer's Mister Thorold i' the church-yaad!"

" Why, my boy Mr. Thorold's been dead and buried this fortnight or more."

" Ah knoo a 'as, but a cooms agen very bad! An' a's theer anow!"

At Scalford, 1853.

Evans, p. 127.

Ghost at Kilncote.—If an account of the *very best ghost* which ever made its appearance in England be worthy of *reappearing* in your magazine, I will raise it. It appeared for several years, but very seldom, only in the church-porch at Kilncote, in Leicestershire, and was discovered by a lady now living, and *then* the rector's wife.

. N.B.—It was not a ghost that would appear *ad libitum*; sometimes it did not appear for four years. The lady determined to approach it; and the nearer she advanced the more confident she was that the substance or shade of a human figure was before her.

" Gentleman's Magazine Library," " Popular Super-
stitions," p. 197.

(From the *Gentleman's Magazine* for 1790, part ii.,
p. 521.)

The Mansion House at Cotes.—Tradition talks of its haunted cellars.

Nichols III. 368.

A rare tract by Philip Stubbes, author of the " Anatomy of Abuses," informs us how in June, 1581, " the devil very strangely appeared to a woman named Joane Bowser, dwelling at Castle

Donington," the incidents of which event are set forth in a long poem.

Kelly's "Notices," p. 114, note.

[The poem is given at length in the "Leicester Chronicle" for March 6th, 1875.   Ed.]

The Bloody Tomb at Hinckley.—Children and strangers used to be taken in April to see the "bloody tears" on the inscription (on this tomb, that of Richard Smith, died April 12th, 1727); and certainly it appeared as if every letter had "gouts of blood, which were not there before," and which in course of time disappeared. People were told how this young man had been killed by a recruiting sergeant in Duck-puddle for some light jest; and yearly this stone cried for vengeance.   (This appearance caused by washing down of friable bits of red sandstone in the wall.)

"Leicester Chronicle," June 20th, 1874.

Apparition.—"Also this same yere (13th Ed. IV.) ther was a voyce, cryenge in the heyre, betwyx Laicetur (Leicester), and Bambury, Upper Dunmothe, and in dyverse other places, herde a long tyme cryinge 'Bowes! Bowes!' which was herde of xl. menne; and some menne saw that he that cryed soo was *a hedles manne;* and many other dyverse tokenes have been schewede in Englande this yere, for amendynge of mennys lyvynge."

"Warkworth's Chronicle," p. 24.

Quoted by Kelly, "Royal Progresses," p. 231.

Haunted Houses.—House near East Gates haunted by the ghost of Mrs. Smalley who died 1727.   The ghost was finally laid by the Vicar of St. Martin's.

See "Throsby's History," p. 183, and "Leicester Chronicle," 28th November, 1874.

Two houses in St. Martin's Churchyard about 1800.   In one of these the bells used to ring without visible or traceable cause.

House in Friar Lane about 1820. (Invisible persons walked about with heavy shoes—origin never detected.)

House in Sanvy Gate about 1860. (No details.)

"Leicester Chronicle," 28th November and 5th December, 1874.

[*See* other instances in the same newspaper for 26th December, 1874, 2nd January, 1875 (two houses at Kibworth), 9th January, 1874 (Earl Shilton), 23rd January, 1875), Snareston Old Hall pulled down about 1835 because nobody would live in it, on account of its being haunted.]

Goblindom at Hinckley.—The moats, or "motts," originally the old fish stews, belonging to the Priory by the "Old Hall," now part of the Vicarage grounds, have gradually disappeared, though they may still be partly traced. In a conversation with our much-respected and venerable ex-sexton, old Tom Paul (eighty-six years old), he remembered the old "motts" well. . . . I also obtained from him a very interesting piece of folk-lore, and which, as a lad, I had often heard talked of, but never could understand before. It was enacted at "the Old Hall" before mentioned. He said he had often heard his mother (who lived to a great age) relate how a child had been flogged to death there, and she remembered hearing its cries, having resided near to or adjoining the church-yard at the time, and this poor child's spirit haunted the place afterwards ; and, in order to "lay the spirit," I understood a certain number of ministers had to be got together in the room where the affair took place, a short religious ceremony was gone through, and they proceeded to "lay the spirit," by exorcising and enticing it into a bottle, securely corked, which was afterwards thrown into the "motts," and I perfectly well remember hearing lads say that at night there could be heard buzzing or humming on the surface.

There was also another very similar story relating to Lash Hill and the pit there, on the foot-road to Burbage. A well-known character who attended the fairs, statutes, and dances, when returning to Burbage at night invariably "fiddled himself" past this spot to appease and charm the spirits there.

> From a paper on "Old Hinckley," by Mr. Thomas
> Harrold: "Transactions of the Leicestershire
> Archæological Society," vi., p. 334.

The Scholar's Bridge Ghost.—About midway between Sapcote and Stoney Stanton, over a rivulet, is a stone arch called *Scholar's Bridge* about which supernatural appearances are said to have been seen; and, though such appearances are generally exploded, the Scholar's Bridge Ghost has been for ages and still continues a nightly terror to many of the inhabitants of both these villages.

> Nichols IV., 899, *see also* 970.

> *See also* Nichols II., 301 (at Redmile Field), III.,
> 800, 801 (Water turned into Blood at Garendon,
> A.D. 1645), III., 1018 (at Shepeshead), III.,
> 1083, 1084 (Healing through miraculous voice
> at Cropston, A.D. 1706), III., 1133 (Ghost of Sir
> George Villiers, Leicestershire, appears to Mr.
> Parker), IV., 549 (before Bosworth Field Battle,
> A.D. 1485), IV., 798 (at Markfield, A.D. 1659).

Mr. Harris said the children were always careful to leave the St. John's Stone before dark, as they thought the fairies came to dance on the stone.

> *See* " Sacred Stones."

Mill-hill (Stoney-Stanton) was formerly famous for fairy rings and fairy dances . . . . about which some old people in the neighbourhood tell many wonderful traditionary tales to this day.

> Nichols IV., 970.

See " Witch-stone."

(e) WITCHCRAFT.

Witchcraft in Leicestershire.—In the accounts for the year 1596
(for the Town of Leicester) is the following entry, illustrating with
horrible significance the superstitious feeling of the age on the
subject of witchcraft, and the judicial murders frequently per-
petrated on the accused :—" Itm. pd. for the charge of meate and
driuke of old Mother Cooke, being kept in the Hall V dayes at the
suite of Mr. Edward Saunders, upon suspicion of witchyre, who
was afterwards removed to the Countye gaiole, and was for the
same arrayned, condemned, and hanged, ijs. vjd."[*]   Twenty years
afterwards (18th July, 1616,) nine unfortunate women were tried
at our assizes before Justice Winch and Serjeant Crew, convicted
and executed for this supposed crime ; [†] and some very curious
particulars relative to their trial are given in a letter from Alderman Robert Heyrick to his brother Sir William, jeweller to
James I.   The letter, slightly altered and modernised in the
orthography by the late Mr. James Thompson, is given in his
" History of Leicester," vol. i., p. 344.

About the same date six others were imprisoned for the same
offence, one of whom died in gaol, and five were set at liberty.
They were examined before the mayor and justices, and a
Dr. Lambe.   The King came to Leicester on the 16th August in
this year, and having personally examined the boy who counter-
feited to have been bewitched, detected the imposture, and the
judges were " discountenanced," and fell into disgrace ; as we
learn by Chamberlain's letters to Sir Dudley Carleton.   This, no
doubt, led to the liberation of the five women (mentioned above)
on the 15th October.   So little evidence was required for con-

---

[*] See Nichols' " Leicestershire," I., 408.   Ed.
[†] *Ibid.,* I., 425.   Ed.

WITCHES.

1650.

1620.

1635.

1717.

demning a witch, that we find by "Scott's Discovery" it was held, "that if she have the witch's mark upon her body it is presumption sufficient for the judge to proceed and give sentence of *death* upon her!" In 1650, as we learn from a manuscript among the Hall papers, this test was tried in this town upon a female named Chettle, who was fortunate enough to escape conviction. She was examined by four of the townswomen, who stated "that they had diligently searched the said Ann Chettle from the crown of her head to the soles of her feet, and found her to be clear of any suspicion." Two years later, however, a warrant was again issued for her apprehension to answer another charge, but the result is not recorded. Several other documents relating to witchcraft are to be found among the Borough MSS. In 1620 a singular charge of sorcery, murder, perjury, and other crimes, was brought by one Christopher Monck, his "familiar," against Gilbert Smith, rector of Swithland, and enforced by petitions to the King and the recorder; and in July, 1635, a poor woman named Agnes Tedsall was tried at the assizes on a charge of having caused the death of Richard Lindsey by witchcraft, but was acquitted. Even so recently as the summer assizes of 1717, Jane Clarke, of Great Wigston, and her son and daughter, were put upon their trial at Leicester for the crime of witchcraft.

> "Leicestershire Notes and Queries," i., pp. 245-7.
> Kelly's "Royal Progresses," p. 367.

1760.

In the *Gentleman's Magazine* for July, 1760, vol. xxx., p. 346, we read : "Two persons concerned in ducking for witches all the poor old women in Glen and Burton Overy were sentenced to stand in the pillory at Leicester.

See another instance which happened at Earl Shilton in Leicestershire, in 1776, in the *Scots' Magazine* for that year, vol. xxxviii., p. 390.

> Brand's "Popular Antiquities," iii., p. 35.

(*See also* post extract from *Journal.*)

The Witches of Belvoir.—On the 11th of March, 16$\frac{18}{19}$ two women, named Margaret and Philippa Flower, were burnt at Lincoln for the alleged crime of witchcraft. With their mother, Joan Flower, they had been confidential servants of the Earl and Countess of Rutland at Belvoir Castle. Dissatisfaction with their employers seems to have gradually seduced these three women into the practice of hidden arts in order to obtain revenge. According to their own confession, they had entered into communion with familiar spirits, by which they were assisted in their wicked designs. Joan Flower, the mother, had hers in the bodily form of a cat, which she called *Rutterkin*. They used to get the hair of a member of the family and burn it; they would steal one of his gloves and plunge it in boiling water, or rub it on the back of Rutterkin, in order to effect bodily harm to its owner. They would also use frightful imprecations of wrath and malice towards the objects of their hatred. In these ways they were believed to have accomplished the death of Lord Rosse, the Earl of Rutland's son, besides inflicting frightful sicknesses upon other members of the family.

It was long before the earl and countess, who were an amiable couple, suspected any harm in these servants, although we are told that for some years there was a manifest change in the countenance of the mother, a diabolic expression being assumed. At length, at Christmas, 1618, the noble pair became convinced that they were the victims of a hellish plot, and the three women were apprehended, taken to Lincoln gaol, and examined. The mother loudly protested innocence, and, calling for bread and butter, wished it might choke her if she were guilty of the offences laid to her charge. Immediately, taking a piece into her mouth, she fell down dead, probably, as we may allowably conjecture, overpowered by consciousness of the contrariety between these protestations and the guilty design which she had entertained in her mind.

Margaret Flower, on being examined, acknowledged that she had stolen the glove of the young heir of the family, and given it to her mother, who stroked Rutterkin with it, dipped it in hot water, and pricked it; whereupon Lord Rosse fell ill and suffered extremely. In order to prevent Lord and Lady Rutland from having any more children, they had taken some feathers from their bed, and a pair of gloves, which they boiled in water mingled with a little blood. In all these particulars, Philippa corroborated her sister. Both women admitted that they had familiar spirits, which came and sucked them at various parts of their bodies; and they also described visions of devils in various forms which they had had from time to time.

Associated with the Flowers in their horrible practices were three other women, of the like grade in life:—Anne Baker, of Bottesford; Joan Willimot, of Goodby; and Ellen Greene, of Stathorne, all in the county of Leicester, whose confessions were much to the same purpose. Each had her own familiar spirits to assist in working out her malignant designs against her neighbours. That of Joan Willimot was called *Pretty*. It had been blown into her mouth by her master, William Berry, in the form of a fairy, and immediately after came forth again and stood on the floor in the shape of a woman, to whom she forthwith promised that her soul should be enlisted in the infernal service. On one occasion, at Joan Flower's house, she saw two spirits, one like an owl, the other like a rat, one of which sucked her under the ear. This woman, however, protested that, for her part, she only employed her spirit in inquiring after the health of persons whom she had undertaken to cure. Greene confessed to having had a meeting with Willimot in the woods, when the latter called two spirits into their company, one like a kitten, the other like a mole, which, on her being left alone. mounted on her shoulders and sucked her under the ears. She had then sent them to bewitch a man and woman who had reviled her, and who accordingly died within a fortnight. Anne Baker seems to have been more of a visionary than any of the rest. She once saw a hand, and heard a voice from the air; she had been visited with a flash of fire; all of them ordinary occurrences in the annals of hallucination. She also had a spirit, but as she alleged, a beneficent one, in the form of a white dog.

*   *   *   *   *

The examinations of these wretched women were taken by magistrates of rank and credit, and, when the judges came to Lincoln, the two surviving Flowers were duly tried and, on their own confessions, condemned to death by the Chief Justice of the Common Pleas, Sir Henry Hobart.

From "The Book of Days," edited by R. Chambers, 1864, vol. i., page 356.

(This account is taken from a pamphlet reprinted in full in Nichols' "Leicestershire," vol. ii., Appendix No. ix., page 69.

See also Nichols, III., 517, quoting Howells' Letters to Sir E. Spencer, 1647.

See also Thomas Wright, "Narratives of Sorcery and Magic," 2nd edition, 1851, vol. ii., pp. 119—125. Ed.)

Two hundred years ago the belief in witchcraft was prevalent throughout the county (Leicestershire). Some horrible transactions took place at Husband's Bosworth, and before that time seven poor creatures were burnt in Woman's Lane, Leicester, from which circumstance it has retained this name till lately.*

Nichols has given a minute account of an affair of this sort at Belvoir Castle. Jane Flower and her daughter were laundresses to the Earl of Rutland, and were dismissed for some misconduct. Soon after, the eldest son, Henry Lord Rosse, fell sick, and it was

---

* In a letter from Alderman Robt. Heyrick to his brother Sir Wm. Heyrick, 18th July, 1616, he says, "We have been occupied five days at the assize in trying witches, nine of which will be executed for bewitching the son, thirteen years old, of Mr. Smythe, of Husband Bosworth. He was shown to the judges and had a fit at the time. Sir Henry Hastings could not hold him. The court ordered the several witches to exercise their spirit upon the boy, when he would neigh like a horse, or mew like a cat, according to the spirit that was within him."—Nichols' "History of Leicestershire," vol. ii., pp. 471, 471*.

WITCHES.   supposed that in revenge these women had bewitched him; especially as the countenance of the mother "had become estranged, and her eyes fiery and hollow, so that no doubt was entertained that she was a witch." After his death, the second son and Lady Catherine were attacked with fits, and it was believed that they also were tormented by Flower and her daughter. They were apprehended about Christmas, 1617, and committed to Lincoln gaol by Sir George Manners, Sir Henry Hastings, and Samuel Flemming, doctor in divinity, upon the depositions of some silly women; tried at the March assizes, before Sir Henry Hobart and Sir Edward Brumley, judges, for the destruction of Henry Lord Rosse with their damnable practices; and they were both hanged at Lincoln.

19TH CEN-   It is not thirty years since the mother of the master of St.
TURY.   George's School, Leicester, a respectable old woman, was dragged through a pond at Wellingboro' on the supposition that she was a witch. Ignorance of a lesser kind still prevails in the illiterate corners of the county. When the ague was common, Headley, a baker near St. Nicholas Church, made a small revenue by selling charms for that complaint; and a workman of ours, Thomas Rask, who lived in the Northgate Street, was constantly applied to for the discovery of things stolen or lost, and found conjuring more profitable than stocking making.

W. Gardiner, "Music and Friends," 1838, vol. i., pp. 406—8.

1776.   "A correspondent has favoured us with the following paragraph, and which we are assured is a fact:—A woman of the parish of Earl-Shilton, in the county of Leicester, has been subject for some years to a disorder resembling that which is said to proceed from the bite of the tarantula, and so astonishing is the ignorance of many, that they imagine that she has been bewitched by an old woman in the neighbouring village of Aston. On Thursday the 20th of June last, the afflicted, her husband, and son, went to the old woman, and, with dreadful imprecations, threatened to destroy her instantly unless she would submit to have blood

drawn from some part of her body, and unless she would give the WITCHES.
woman a blessing, and remove her disorder; the son, who is a
soldier, drew his sword, and pointing to her breast, swore he
would plunge it into her heart if she did not immediately comply;
when the old woman had gone through this ceremony they went
off; but the person not being cured, they collected a great
number of people, and on Monday last returned to Aston,
pretending to have a warrant to justify their proceedings; then,
with uncommon brutality, they took the poor old creature from her
house, stripped her quite naked, and, after tying her hands and
legs together, threw her into a horse-pond. She was then taken
out, and in this shameful condition exhibited for the sport of an
inhuman mob. As she did not sink in the water, they concluded
that she was really a witch, and several returned on the following
day, determined to discipline her in this cruel manner until they
should put an end to her wretched existence; the posse was not
deemed sufficiently strong, so that she escaped for that time; . . .
the consideration of the old woman being more than 80 years of
age, of her being a pauper and friendless . . . render it the
duty of magistrates . . . to exert themselves to bring to condign
punishment these atrocious offenders."

Leicester and Nottingham Journal, July 6th, 1776.
[<i>See also</i> Nichols, IV., 778. Ed.]</div>

From the diary of Humphrey Michel, 1707-11

"June 11, 1709, being St. Barnabas' Festival and Whitsun 1709.
Eve, one Thomas Holmes, of Horninghold, a labourer, was dowsed
three times for a witch, and did not sink, but swam, though his
hands and feet and head were all tyed fast together; and all this
was done in the Dungeon Pit in Blaston, before 500 people (they
say), and by commutation of punishment for stealing Mr. Atkin's
malt."

"June 17, being Whitsun week, one Elizabeth Ridgway and
Jane Barlow, of Horninghold, were both by consent dowsed for

WITCHES.   witches, and did not sink, but swam, though their hands and feet were tyed together—before some thousands of people at the Dungeon Pit in Blaston lordship."

"June 18.   The said Jane Barlow, 40 years old, would be dowsed again to clear herself, but in the great close pond, because she said that was not enchanted as Dungeon Pit (she said) was ; and yet, in the sight of many hundreds of people and myself, she did not sink there but swam again, though she was ty'd as before ; and one Mary Palmer, her sister, a cripple from her cradle, almost 42 years old, was dowsed there for a witch several times, and, though bound hands and feet, did not swim, but sank immediately, like a stone, before us all."

"Aug. 15, 1709.   One ffrances Sharp, the wife of Thomas Sharp, was buryed, and was in all probability bewitched to death by one Widow Ridgway ; for the other confessed that the said Ridgway appeared to her in very terrible shapes, and before she dyed she neither ate nor drank of eleven days, but said she could have done both very heartily but that the little thing in her bosom told her she must do neither ; and while the white witch of Kibworth, one Clow, had ordered a charm to be sewed, and kept it in her shift about her bosom, she did eat and drink, but when she scratched it away, she never ate nor drank more.   Witnesses, her own sister, her sister's daughter, &c."

"Oct. 2, 1709.   A wench of the widow Barlow, a supposed witch, went out of the church when I had named and read my text, Deut., chap. 18, where is the word 'witch.' "

"Transactions of the Architectural and Archæol. Societies," vol. i., pp. 377, 378.

Wymeswold.—It is commonly believed in this town, that about 80 or 100 years ago, there were several witches, of whom the old inhabitants relate strange stories.

Nichols, III., 504.

See " Witch-stone."

(*f*) LEECHCRAFT.

(1) To rub them three times with the rind of *stolen bacon.* WART
The rind was then to be nailed up on some outside wall, and, CHARMS.
as it dried up, the wart would dry up likewise.

From Mrs. J. D. Paul.

(2) I remember in Leicestershire seeing the following charm
employed for the removal of a number of warts on my brother, a
child about five years old. In the month of April or May he was
taken to an *ash-tree* by a lady, who carried also a paper of fresh
pins : one of these was first stuck through the bark, and then
pressed through the wart, until it produced pain; it was then
taken out and stuck into the tree. Each wart was thus treated, a
separate pin being used for each. The warts certainly disappeared in about six weeks. I saw the same tree a year or two
ago, when it was very thickly studded over with old pins, each the
index of a cured wart.

> T. J., "Notes and Queries," vii., 81; "Choice
> Notes," ("Folk-Lore"), p. 252.
> [*See* "Folk-Lore Record," vol. i., pp. 158 and 224;
> Northall's "English Folk Rhymes," p. 136.
> Ed.]

(3) Get a *black snail*, rub it on the wart, then stick it on
a thorn until it dies.

From a native of West Leicestershire.

(4) Take the pod of a *broad-bean*, rub it on the wart, then
either bury it or throw it over the shoulder without looking
back.

From a native of Woodville, near Ashby-le-la-Zouch.

2 2

WART
CHARMS.   (5) Cut an *apple* in halves, rub the wart with the cut parts, bury the apple in a secret place ; as it decays, so will the wart.

From a native of Woodhouse.

(6) It is believed by the peasantry that a sanatory power is imparted to the *wedding ring*, so that any growth like a wart on the skin may be removed by rubbing a wedding ring upon them.

I have known this cure applied several times, in the case of a stye in the eye.

From Mrs. J. D. Paul.

See also under " Witch-stone."

CHURCH-
YARD
MOULD.   *Churchyard Mould a cure for Rheumatism.*—" This day a very odd experiment was tried upon a young man about twenty-five years of age, who was much afflicted with the rheumatism.   He was ordered to be buried in the earth for two hours, naked, his face only uncovered ; which operation was accordingly performed, and he lay the time.   The man says he feels himself much better ; it is said he is to be buried again to-morrow for three hours."

From the *Leicester and Nottingham Journal*,
May 13th, 1775.

VARIOUS.   *Docks and Nettles.*—When a lad is stung by a nettle, he generally searches for a dock (*rumex obtusifolius*), with the leaves of which he whips the part affected, repeating the words

" In, dock ! out, nettle ! "

a word with every blow.

Evans, p. 139.
(*See* Northall, p. 131.   Ed.)

Spiders.—" Being in the country in the vacation time not many years since at Lindly, in Leicestershire, my father's house, I first observed this amulet, of a spider in a nutshell lapped up in silk, CHARMS. &c., so applied for an ague by my mother."

> Burton, "Anatomy of Melancholy," part ii., section 5, sub-section 6.

Burton adds a note, "Mistress Dorothy Burton, she died 1629." (*See* Evans, p. 183.

> Black, "Folk-Medicine," Folk-Lore Society, 1883, p. 59. Ed.)

Swallowing Shot.—A recognised remedy for the "raisin' o' the loights" (*i.e.* heart-burn).

> Evans, p. 186.

Fried Mice are an infallible cure for whooping cough.

> (So in N.E. Lincolnshire : Black, "Folk-Medicine," p. 159. Ed.)

Fried mice eaten for quinsy.

> From a Leicestershire servant.

Charm for Whooping-Cough.—To seat the patient on a donkey with its (*sic*) face towards its tail, and give him a *roast mouse* to eat. It is hardly necessary to say that he must not know what he is eating. The same practice has prevailed in Leicester-shire. . . . ."

> Henderson, " Folk-Lore of Northern Counties," p. 144.

Silverweed (*Potentilla anserina*).—Used in Leicestershire for removing marks of small-pox.

> " Folk-Lore Record," i., p. 185, quoting Hardwicke's " Science Gossip," ii., p. 163.

Pegging Calves.—The custom of " pegging " calves or yearlings " for the black leg," which in my remembrance was so common as to be almost universal, is now rapidly dying out. It was performed either in the ear or the dewlap. In the former case, a hole was either punched or burnt with a hot iron through the ear. generally on the first Friday after the birth of the calf. In the latter, a hole was burnt through both skins of the dewlap when the animal was a year or sometimes two years old. In both cases a twist of horsehair about five inches long was inserted through the hole and secured with a wooden peg at each end. This twist was moved backwards and forwards once a week like a seton, and occasional dressings were applied. The disease itself, called in Sussex a " pook," is a congestion of the blood-vessels of the leg, which entirely discolours the flesh, and is incurable. An animal attacked by it is called a " black-leg," a term meta- phorically applied to the victim of mortal disease.

Evans, p. 210.

Charm against Drunkenness.—" An almanac for 1678, calculated by John Goldsmith, in which were some curious manuscripts notes, receipts, &c., among which the following rather singular one :—

" 'Take the lungs of an hog ; roast it ; whosoever eateth thereof fasting shall not be drunk that day, how liberally soever hee takes his drinks.' "

" Transactions of Leicestershire Architectural and
Archæological Societies," vol. iii., p. 13.

Charming for frost, whooping-cough, fits, &c.—The operator, generally an old woman, draws a circle round the sufferer's face nine times with her fore-finger, pausing each time at the centre of the forehead and the chin, her lips moving silently during the performance. (My friends remember their younger sister being charmed for whooping-cough. The house was made scrupulously clean and tidy, the children were dressed in their best, with clean white pinafores, they sat on stools and were not allowed to utter a word while the old woman charmed the baby that the mother held on her knee.)

(It would be very interesting to discover the words of the charm, but the charm was supposed to be of non-effect, if the words were known—not to be a charm in fact ; probably they were transmitted from mother to daughter as a treasure to be secretly guarded, and may now be irrecoverably lost, but I shall still prosecute inquiries, hoping to gain some light on the subject.)

From Miss S. A. Squires.

In the early part of the reign of Charles the First, before he began to quarrel with his subjects about religion. he used to make tours through the country. In coming to a large town he would announce that persons afflicted with the king's evil, upon being properly recommended, might approach him and receive a cure by the Royal touch.*

Our Leicester historian, Throsby, who was clerk of St. Martin's, informs us that till of late years there hung up in the vestry a Royal manifesto, stating that all persons, on procuring a certificate from the churchwarden or minister, might repair to London and receive the benefit of the Royal touch.†

This proclamation emanated from a court held at Whitehall, when not less than twenty of the privy councillors were present. It further ordered that the times of healing should be from the feast of Allhallows till a week before Christmas, and after Christmas till the 15th day of March ; and, when his Majesty

---

* When King Charles was at Belvoir, his chamberlain, Lord Pembroke, wrote to the High Sheriff of Staffordshire the King's commands, that no fern should be burnt at the time he was about to visit them, as he understood it brought down rain ; not doubting his people would consider his Majesty's comfort, they would forbear all burning of fern till he had passed through that county, and would be ready to observe his Majesty's commands.

† Charles the Second, in five years, touched more than twenty-three thousand persons ; the bishops assisted with a sort of heathenish service for the occasion. This superstitious ceremony was performed in public, and we are told that, as soon as prayers were ended, the Duke of Buckingham brought a towel, and the Earl of Pembroke a basin and ewer, and after they had made obeisance to his Majesty, kneeled down till he had washed. [The form of service and other particulars may be found in Beckett's "Touching for the Cure of the King's Evil," London, 1722. Ed.]

KING'S
EVIL.

shall think fit to go any progress, he will be pleased to appoint such other times for healing as shall be convenient. The bishops were charged to see that this act for performing this great charity should be hung up in all churches.

> From "Music and Friends," by William Gardiner, 1838, vol. i., p. 409.
> *See also* under "Witchcraft."

(*g*) MAGIC AND DIVINATION.

THE KEY
IN THE
BIBLE.

Take the house door-key, and place the ward in the Bible over "The Song of Solomon," ch. viii. ver. vii. Close the book, leaving the ring of the key out at the top; tie the garter of the right leg tightly round the Bible, then place the third finger of each hand under the ring of the key, and hold the Bible suspended while repeating these words: "Many waters cannot quench love, neither can the floods drown it. If a man would give all the substance of his house for love, it would utterly be contemned."

If the Bible turn round, the one who holds it will marry; if it continues stationary, she will remain single.

After this formula has been gone through, if the Bible and key are placed under the pillow, the sleeper will dream of his or her future partner.

After placing the key in the Bible if you wish to ascertain the initial letter of the future husband's name, repeat, "If my true love's name begins with A, turn Bible, turn key," and so on through all the letters of the alphabet until the Bible and key turn.

> From a native of Woodhouse.
> (*See* Northall, p. 124.   Ed.)

DREAMS.

Before retiring to rest, place the shoes in the form of a T, the toe of one touching the instep of the other, and if you repeat DREAMS. these words you will dream of your true love—

> " I set my shoes in the form of a T,
> Hoping to dream who my true love is to be ;
> The shape of his body the colour of his hair,
> The Sunday clothes that he does wear."

Another version—

> " I set my shoes in the form of a T,
> Hoping this night my true love to see,
> Not in costly apparel or lordly array,
> But in the clothes he wears every day."

Another version—

> " T, T, T, as I set thee,
> Hoping my true love to see,
> Whether I sleep or whether I wake,
> I hope my true love to see."

[See Northall, p. 120. Ed.]

Cut the *finger-nails* and place them under the pillow, will dream of the future husband.

To dream of a wedding is a sign of a death.

To dream of a death, a sign of a wedding.

> From two ladies, aged seventy-two and seventy-four respectively, natives of Woodhouse.

Dragon's Blood.—Buy a pennyworth of dragon's blood from a DRAGON'S chemist, sprinkle the powder in the fire any night when the clock BLOOD. is striking twelve, and your future husband or wife will appear.

(When Mrs. ——— was a girl she tried this charm one night while the clock was striking twelve, and upon turning from the fire she saw the figure of a man, resembling the one who afterwards became her husband, become embodied out of the air, then gradually fade away. She was so terrified that she never attempted

DRAGON'S
BLOOD.

the charm again.   Mrs. ——— is firmly convinced that she saw this apparition.)

[*See* Northall, p. 157.   Ed.]

Dragon's Blood and Quicksilver.—If a young girl has lost the affection of her lover, she can regain it by throwing dragon's blood and quicksilver into the fire as the clock strikes twelve at midnight and at the same time wishing for his return to her.

From Miss S. A. Squires.

LOVE
CHARMS.

Love Charms.—There is still a stout belief in the power of a person who makes use of a love charm to draw that person to her side.   A lady (aged 70) told me that when she was young a young man, whose affection she did not reciprocate, came to her father's house one evening and asked her if she had been "trying a charm." She indignantly repudiated the idea, but he would not accept her word.   "You must have done so," he insisted, "for not all the powers of hell could have kept me from you to-night."

From Miss S. A. Squires.

THE CROSS.

If a fire does not burn well, and you want to draw it up, you should set the poker across the hearth, with the fore part leaning across the top bar of the grate, and you will have a good fire if you wait long enough; but you must not be unreasonable, and refuse to give time for the charm to work.   For a charm it is, the poker and top bar combined forming a cross, and so defeating the malice of the gnomes, who are jealous of our possession of their subterranean treasure; or else of the witches and demons who preside over smoky chimneys.

From Mrs. J. D. Paul.

See *also* under "Festival Customs" (Miscellaneous) and "Animal Superstitions" (Birds).

MID-
SUMMER
EVE
CHARMS.

Midsummer Eve.—At midnight if a young girl went into the garden and plucked a sage-leaf each time the clock struck until the twelfth note had sounded, the apparition of her future husband would appear.   If the girl is not destined to be married a coffin

will appear. My informant said that when she was in service in MID-
the country the cook and housemaid, her fellow servants, tried SUMMER
this charm. The housemaid saw a coffin; she has not been EVE
married. The cook saw her lover. This same lover came to see CHARMS.
his betrothed as early as five o'clock the next morning, declaring
that he had not been able to rest during the night, and that he
was compelled to seek his affianced as soon as it was light.

Miss S. A. Squires.

Midsummer Eve.—If a young girl wished to see her future
husband, she would lay the table for twelve guests on Midsummer
Eve, and invite ten of her friends, each of whom would take a
place at the table, the girl who desired to see her future husband
occupying the seat next to the vacant chair. They would sit in
silence with their eyes fixed upon their plates. If one of them
spoke the spell was broken. The doors of the house were wide
open. When the clock struck twelve an apparition appeared—
the future husband—who took possession of the place reserved for
him at the board by the side of his prospective wife. Sometimes
instead of the husband a funeral procession passed through the
room, and the corpse would take a seat next to the girl, who
would die before the end of the year.

From Woodhouse Eaves. Miss S. A. Squires.

(One old lady told me that she tried this "charm" when she
was a young girl. She and others sat silent for hours. When
the clock struck twelve they heard footsteps approaching, whereupon they became so terrified that they all sprang up and rushed
to their respective bedrooms.—S. A. S.)

Wedding Ring.—A large mince-pie, in which a wedding-ring WEDDING
and a button have been placed, the upper crust marked in squares RINGS.
with a knife before cooking. When served at table, whoever has
the piece containing the wedding-ring will be married first of
the company, the one to whom the button falls will be an old
maid—if a gentleman, a bachelor.

From a native of Woodhouse.

The Wise Woman of Leicester.—*See* Henderson, p. 244.

See also under "Animal Superstitions" [Birds], "Superstitions Generally."

(*h*) SUPERSTITIONS GENERALLY.

SUPER-
STITIONS.

If you break two things you will break a third.

Many persons on the first appearance of the new moon will turn the money in their pockets for luck.

If it rain on S. Swithin's day it will rain for forty days.

To see the "old moon in the arms of the new one" is reckoned a sign of fine weather.

Jacob's Ladder.—The streaks of light often seen when the sun shines through broken clouds are believed to be pipes reaching into the sea, and the water is supposed to be drawn up through them into the clouds, ready to be discharged in the shape of rain. This phenomenen is sometimes called "Jacob's Ladder," also "the sun drawing water," and is considered a sure sign of rain.

Evans, p. 177.

Infant's Caul is worn as a safeguard against drowning. (Sailors often give a high price for one.)

It is lucky to put on any article of dress, particularly stockings, inside out; but if you wish the omen to hold good, you must continue to wear the reversed portion of your attire in that condition till the regular time comes for pulling it off—that is either bedtime or cleaning yourself. If you set it right you will "change the luck." It will be of no use to put on anything with SUPER- STITIONS. the wrong side out on purpose.

The clothes of the dead will never wear long.

If you would have good luck, you must wear something new on Easter Sunday.

From Mrs. J. D. Paul.

It is very unlucky to fold up your clothes carefully at night. The reason assigned is that by so doing you fold up the day's sins with them.

From a Leicestershire domestic servant.

There is a doggrel * concerning cutting *the nails*, but the only part of this I have heard here is a variant of the last line, " Cut them on Sunday, and you'll have the devil with you all the week."

I well remember being scolded by a servant for cutting my nails on Sunday, because it was " buttering the devil's pie-dish."

From Mrs. J. D. Paul.

[See Northall, 172. Ed.]

Mothers-Stone or Mothering-Stone, i.e., conglomerate; " pudding- stone ;" " breeding-stone " (*Herts*). The belief that stones grow in size by degrees is almost universal, and the small pebbles found in conglomerates are generally recognised as *ora*, which under favourable auspices will ultimately be developed into boulders.

Evans. p. 196.

[I have found it all but impossible to eradicate this belief from one Leicester boy's mind. Ed.]

Cows.—A mite towards an history of the force of imagination in brutes : A Mr. William Chamberlain, an intelligent farmer and

* See Chambers' " Book of Days," vol. ii., pp. 321-2.

grazier at Ayleston, in Leicestershire, had six cows that cast calf, occasioned, he thinks, by the miscarriage of *one* in the same pasture, by a kind of contagious sympathy, which common experience, he says, has established as a fact.—W. B.

> *Gentleman's Magazine*, 1784, i., 258.
>
> ("Gentleman's Magazine Library," "Popular Superstitions," ed. G. L. Gomme. Elliot Stock, 1884, p. 196.)

Dandelions.—The head of the dandelion covered with seeds is called a clock. The time of day is supposed to be ascertainable by gathering one of these and blowing at it, the number of puffs required to clear off all the seeds corresponding with the hour.

> Evans, p. 124.

If you drop a knife, a male visitor will come to the house.
If you drop a spoon, a female visitor will come.

> From a Leicestershire domestic servant.

Superstitions generally.—A number of those general superstitions which are to be found all over England are common in Leicestershire. Help to salt, help to sorrow. Spill the salt—a sign of bad luck; you must throw a pinch over left shoulder. Two teaspoons in a cup at the same time—a sign of a wedding. A tablespoon on the floor—a sign of a quarrel. Crossing of knives at table —very unlucky. You mustn't see the new moon for the first time through a window. Turn your money over when you see a new moon. Hair should be cut on first seeing a new moon, to make it grow. Unlucky to leave a white cloth on a table over night, &c., &c.

Death Signs.—Ticking of the death-spider. The continuous howling of a dog. When a clock in a house, at noon or midnight, strikes *thirteen*. If thirteen sit down to dinner, one will die before the end of the year. When apple-trees bloom out of season there will be a death in the family. A winding-sheet in the candle. A

swarm of mice in the house. A coffin-shaped hole in the loaf. To
hear the cock crow at night. To dream of riding in a cart and to
be greased with bacon.

Signs of a Wedding.—To fall upstairs. If a live coal fall out of
the fire near to your feet. If four people meet and cross hands, to
shake hands.

New Moons.—" You may see as many new moons at once
through a silk handkerchief as there are years before you will
marry."

"Notes and Queries," "Choice Notes" (Folk-
Lore), p. 244.

The person who sees the new moon for the first time through
glass will break some crockery.

The first time you see the *new moon*, bow three times and wish,
the wish will be fulfilled.

Bad Luck.—To break a looking-glass will bring seven years' bad
luck. Nothing will succeed that is begun on a Friday. To open
an umbrella in the house. To put an umbrella on the table. To
put the bellows on the table. To be married in black (a lady).
To let a baby look in a mirror before it is twelve months old. To
walk under a ladder. To see the new moon through glass. To
turn the bed over on Sundays will bring bad luck all the week.
To turn the salt over. To pass another person on the stairs. To
return to a house after having just left it. To boast about anything will cause the luck to turn relating to that particular object;
to prevent that, knock under the table. To keep evergreen
decorations longer than six weeks after Christmas.

Good Luck.—To find a horse-shoe.

A spark in the candle indicates that the one to whom it points
is about to receive a letter. Knock the candlestick, repeating the
days of the week from the present day, and at the mention of

whichever one it falls—say Monday, Tuesday—upon that day will
the letter be received.

Wish when you eat the *first mince-pie.* As many mince-pies as
one eats (each at a different house) so many happy months will he
have in a year.

If one person begins to pour out the tea, and another takes
charge of the tea-pot to finish, there will be a birth in the family
within twelve months.

If a black object, like a thickened spider-web, hangs on the
bar, it indicates that a stranger will call at the house.

From Miss S. A. Squires.

(*See* Northall, p. 124. Ed.)

If a maid gets her clothes very wet when she is washing, she
will have a drunken husband.

When a maiden's apron string comes untied, her lover is thinking about her.

> " If the garter tightens the love heightens,
>   If the garter slackens, the love backens."

Folding carpets after shaking them ; if the last fold is perfectly
even with the others, the folder will be married within the
year.

If a piece of bread and butter falls from the hand to the floor
with the buttered surface downwards, the one who drops it will
have no new dress that year.

A piece of stalk, a sweetheart, floating on the top of the tea,
take it out, place it on the top of the closed fingers of the left
hand, then, with the closed fingers of the right—the little finger
end—beat the stalk, repeating at each stroke: 1st, this year;
2nd, next year; 3rd, sometime; 4th, never; at whichever word
the stalk adheres to the right hand that will foretell the period of
marriage.

A Stranger on the Bar.—Kneel on the hearth, clap the hands close to the little black flag, if the day be Monday, repeat Monday (clap), Tuesday, and so on, through the days of the week; if the "stranger" drop from the bar at the mention of, say Wednesday, then a visitor will appear at the house on that day. (The draught caused by the sudden meeting of the hands will sometimes dislodge the "stranger" from the bar.)

From a native of Woodhouse.

If one who is shelling peas discovers a pod containing nine *perfect* peas, and places it on the lintel of the outer door, the first man who crosses the threshold will become her husband; or she can put the pod containing the peas in the place mentioned, and repeat the name of another person who is in the house (Mary for instance), the first man who enters will become Mary's husband.

(In two instances known to my informant this came true, of course, and caused much after comment and joking.)

The rind of an apple taken off without a fracture, and swung three times round the head of the person who is trying the charm and thrown over the left shoulder, will form the initial letter of the name of her future husband.

The loss of an ornament in the form of a horse-shoe, worn as a charm, reverses the good luck previously enjoyed by the owner.

A horse-shoe nailed on a door renders the evil power of a witch that may enter of non-effect.

A tablespoonful of lead melted and poured into a glass of water, will form a representation of the future home (after marriage) of the one who tries the charm.

Gifts (white spots) on the finger nails. A gift on the thumb is sure to come, a gift on the finger is sure to linger. Thumb a gift; first finger, a friend; second, a fool; third, a bearing; fourth, a letter to come or a journey to go.

[See Northall, p. 171.   Ed.]

A Fortune Trifle.—Put in the trifle, a wedding-ring, a silver thimble, and a threepenny piece. The one who gets the wedding-ring will be married within the year, the one who has the three-penny piece will be a bachelor, and the one to whose lot the thimble falls will be an old maid.

If a young girl writes the names of four gentlemen, each of whom has paid her marked attentions, on a laurel leaf, and places it in water in her bedroom at night, the name which is most legible in the morning is the name of the one she will marry.

From Mrs. Roberts.

A spike of grass gathered in a meadow, with small clusters on either side and one at the top. Anyone wishing to ascertain when he, or she, will marry, will touch a tuft on alternate sides until the terminal tuft is reached, saying : this year, next year, sometime, never (repeat). Position of the future husband : rich man, poor man, beggar man, thief. Trade : tinker, tailor, soldier, sailor. To be married in : silk, satin, muslin, delaine. To drive to church in : coach, carriage, wheelbarrow, cart.

(This is a frequent pastime with country children when playing in the fields.)

Fruit stones collected on the plate after eating jam or stewed fruit, to 1st stone, this year; 2nd, next year; 3rd, sometime : 4th, never. Period of marriage.

From Miss S. A. Squires.

Thedingworth.—It is believed that, if the church clock strikes during sermon, someone in the village will die within the week. An instance occurred recently, and the death duly followed.

From Mr. G. R. Kirwan.

Superstition against a King entering Leicester.—In Rishanger's "Chronicle of the Barons' Wars,"* the superstition is thus mentioned :—

"Now, the King, having taken Northampton, marched towards Leicester, where he was entertained, which town no King before him had presumed to enter, or even to behold—certain persons superstitiously preventing it."

The existence of this curious belief, which, as we have abundantly seen, was far from being founded on fact, is also recorded by other ancient writers, among whom may be mentioned Matthew of Westminster and Thomas Wykes.

After a fruitless search for any particulars which might elucidate its origin, or explain the terrible consequences expected to ensue from a disregard of the superstition, and after an unsuccessful enquiry on the subject in "Notes and Queries," the only conclusion at which we can arrive is that it probably owes its origin to Geoffrey of Monmouth's narrative of the legendary woes of King Leir, the founder of Leicester—his work having been very popular in the Middle Ages ; for we find that a similar belief existed with respect to the city of Oxford, and which owed its origin to a monkish legend. . . . . . There is a third city with which a similar superstition was connected—that of Lincoln.

Kelly, " Royal Progresses," p. 112.

---

* Edited by Dr. J. O. Halliwell-Phillips for the Camden Society. The passage in the original is as follows :—" Rex autem, capta Northampton, Leycestr. tendens in ea hospitatus est, quam nullis regni præter eum etiam videre, prohibentibus quibusdam superstitiose præsumpsit " (p. 26).

Part II.

TRADITIONAL CUSTOMS.

(a) FESTIVAL CUSTOMS.

NEW YEAR. *New Year Gifts.*—A custom of offering New Year's gifts to the Lord of Beaumanor was long observed among the tenantry; it is now, I believe, laid aside.

Potter, p. 87.

1607-8. "Item the said Last daye of December, p^d for vj gallons one quart of Sacke, & a Rundlet for it, sent to Sr Augustyne Nicolls, knight (of Foston), S^rgiant at Lawe our Recorder for a New Yeeres giefte . . . . . . **xxvj^s. viij^d.**

Extracted from the Chamberlain's Accounts for the
Borough of Leicester by Mr. W. Kelly.

First Foot.—If the first visitor who enters the house on New Year's Day is a *dark man*, there will be good luck in the house for the year.

Mrs. Billson, native of country near Bagworth, assures me that she has a vivid recollection of her mother and her grandmother not permitting anyone to cross their threshold on New Year's morning until a *dark man* had first entered the house. They regarded it as particularly unlucky for a woman to be the first visitor. We reckoned this back as far as 130 years.

From Miss S. A. Squires.

Shittles.—Lozenge-shaped buns, with currants and carraways, given to children and old people on Valentine's Day.—I (Rev. C. Wordsworth, Glaston Rectory, near Uppingham) saw one last year (1879), but this was said to have become uncommon as a gift, though still commonly sold. The bakers' name is "Valentine-buns," and they are still carried round for sale, as hot-cross-buns are on Good Friday elsewhere.

VALEN-
TINE'S
DAY.

Evans, p. 298.

The same custom is still observed at Market Overton, Rutland, where the buns are called "Plum Shuttles" (pronounced Shittles), being of an oval shape, like a weaver's shuttle.

"Leicestershire Notes and Queries," iii., 159.

A Valentine at Beaumanor.—On my second visit, three hundred children with happy faces were on their way to Beaumanor.

On inquiring the object of this assemblage of healthy-looking rustics, I learnt that they "were going to Beaumanor for a valentine;" where, I understood, each child received a penny, and a halfpenny on their returning, from Miss Watkinson. . . . This custom has long since been observed here.

In 1743 there were only thirty recipients.

Potter, page 87.

[*See also* Nichols, III., 115. Ed.]

Pancake Bell is rung in the parishes of Ashby-de-la-Zouch, Aylestone, Barrow-on-Soar, Belgrave, Belton, Billesdon, Bottesford, Broughton Astley, Burton Overy, Church Langton, Claybrook, Cosby, Coston, Dalby Magna, Diseworth, Evington, Fleckney, Frowlesworth, Glen Magna, Hallaton, Hinckley, Hose, Houghton-on-the-Hill, Hungerton, Kegworth, Kibworth, Knipton, St. Margaret's Leicester, St. Mary's Leicester, St. Mark's Leicester, All Saints' Loughborough, Lutterworth, Market Bosworth (now discontinued), Markfield, Muston, Nailston, Oadby, Peckleton, Rearsby (now discontinued), Rothley, Sapcote, Seale (Over) Sharnford, Sheepshed, Sibson, Sileby, South Kilworth, Syston,

SHROVE-
TIDE.

Thedingworth, Thurnby (now discontinued), Woodhouse, Wymondham.

> From North's "Church Bells of Leicestershire,"
> pp. 134-309.

Pancake Bell is rung in the parishes of Ashwell, Ayston, Belton, Braunstone (discontinued), Caldecot, Empingham (discontinued), Glaston, Langham, Lyddington, Manton (discontinued), Market Overton, Morcot (discontinued), Oakham, Ryhall, Seaton (discontinued), Teigh, Thistleton, Wardley, Whissendine.

> From North's "Church Bells of Rutland," pp. 118-166.

At Belgrave, the Pancake-Bell is rung by the oldest apprentice in the parish.

> North's "Church Bells of Leicestershire," pp. 118, 144.

At Belton, Shrove Tuesday is kept as a general holiday.

> *Ib.*, p. 145.

At Hinckley, Shrove Tuesday was kept to some extent, until recently, as a holiday. After the Pancake-Bell had been rung, then anyone was allowed, on payment of one penny, to go into the belfry and ring the bells. (Discontinued.)

> *Ib.*, pp. 119, 186.
> [*See* Nichols IV., 682, note. Ed.]

Shrove Tuesday is celebrated in Hinckley by a general game of shuttlecock and battledore, which is a very novel and amusing sight to a stranger.

> *Leicester Chronicle*, Feb. 12, 1842.

In Newark was held an annual fair on Shrove Tuesday, and there was then formerly practised in its fullest extent the barbarous custom of throwing at cocks, when some were tied to a stake, and others left at liberty in consequence of their being trained, to shift for themselves from the well-aimed blows of boys and men, who, with bludgeons, by giving a certain sum of money (generally two pence) had six throws.

From Mr. William Kelly, F.S.A., F.R.H.S.

The abolition of throwing at cocks on Shrove Tuesday was begun, and nearly effected, in Mr. Oldham's mayoralty (1783-4).

Nichols, I., 450.

On Shrove Tuesday the children in Leicester begin or used to begin to play at shuttlecock and battledore in the streets and open places.

Ed.

On Shrove Tuesday a bell rings at noon, which is meant as a signal for the people to begin frying their pancakes; nor must I omit to observe that by many of the parishioners due respect is paid to Mothering Sunday.

Macaulay's " Claybrook," p. 121.
Brand's " Antiquities," i., 112.
Dyer's " British Popular Customs " (Bohn), p. 80.

We have had, until within the last twenty years or so, a "pancake bell" rung at noon on Shrove Tuesday. This has been discontinued only within my own incumbency.

Rev. C. H. Newmarch, in " Leicestershire Notes and Queries," i., 275.

Shrove Tuesday has long been considered a holiday by the young people; in several parishes in this diocese they were allowed on that day to jangle the bells . . . in other places the women-folk were allowed to do the same.

North's " Church Bells of Rutland," pp. 103-104.

Barring Out.—An old custom of obtaining the half holiday by "barring the master out of school" survived at Frisby-on-the-

2 3 *

Wreke until within the last forty years. The method of pro-
cedure was to entice the master by a preconcerted manœuvre
outside the door of the school-house, and then turn the key upon
him. The youngsters within would then commence to shout
vigorously :—

> " Pardon, master, pardon,
> Pardon in a pin,
> If you don't give a holiday,
> We won't let you in."

or :—

> " Pardon, master, pardon,
> Pardon in a spout,
> If you don't give a holiday,
> We'll all keep you out."

No Leicestershire schoolmaster is now " pardoned out of school "
when the Pancake Bell rings at Shrovetide, but in many places
children are allowed a little special license at that season, and may
be seen playing in fields (possibly the old common land of the
village) usually deemed sacred from such intrusion.

"Bygone Leicestershire," p. 119.

See also under " Local Customs." [Whipping Toms.]

Mothering Sunday.—Mid-lent or Laetare Jerusalem Sunday, when
all parishioners were formerly expected to make their Lenten
offerings at their Mother Church. It is now a family festival,
when the scattered members of the village household expect leave
to go home for the day to eat veal and furmety with their mothers
in the flesh.

Evans, p. 196.

Payment of Eggs to Vicar.—Croughton *v.* Blake.—This was
an action to determine whether the vicar of Melton had a right
to tithe in kind from the township of Eye Kettleby, a part of the
parish. . . . . Mr. Hawley was called to prove that it was
customary to pay eggs to the vicar on Good Friday, two for a

hen and three for a cock, but these, he said, were never called tithes.

Leicestershire Chronicle and Mercury, August 5th, 1843.

The Vicar of Garthorpe hath also tithe pigs, geese, ducks, chickens, apples, pears, &c., and eggs, as usual in other places, on Good Friday, two eggs for a hen, and three for a cock.

Nichols, II., 191.
So at Claybrook. Nichols, IV., 112. Ed.

Easter Eve.—The Holy Fire.—On Easter Even, too, the hallowed fire was lighted:— **EASTER EVE.**

1544. Pd. for charcole on East. even . . ijd.

1545-6. Item for a stryke of charcole on Easter even . . ijd.

And again in 1558:—

Pd. for a stryke of charcole for the hallowed fyer . . vd.*

The hallowed or holy fire was kindled in the church porch on the morning of Holy Saturday (Easter Eve), and was obtained from the sun by means of a crystal or burning-glass, if the morning was bright; if not, a flint and steel were used. This fire was blessed by the priest, and from it the Paschal Candle, the lamps in the church, and the candles on the altar, were lighted— the latter at mass on Holy Saturday, which was anciently performed immediately after midnight, that is, early on Saturday morning—and which was in honour of our Lord's Resurrection. This service, however, was in process of time allowed to take place by anticipation on Saturday morning. The people, too, took home with them (according to Dr. Rock) a light from the sanctuary, and the hearth that had been allowed to become cold and brandless then became warm and bright once more, and the

---

* [The following extracts from the Churchwardens' accounts of St. Mary's, Leicester, have been made by Mr. William Kelly.

    1494. Paid for coles for the holy fire. 1½d.

    1495. Rec. on Pace-day for the waste of torches. 4s.

    1502. Paid for coles for the holy fire. 1d. Ed.]

evening candle shone brightly again with a flame from the new-hallowed fire.

> "A Chronicle of the Church of St. Martin, in
> Leicester," by Thomas North. (London: Bell
> and Daldy, 1866), p. 59.

EASTER.

Hunting the Hare at Leicester.—" It had long been customary on Easter Monday for the mayor and his brethren, in their scarlet gowns, attended by their proper officers, in form, to go to a certain close, called Black-Annis'-Bower Close,* parcel of, or bordering upon, Leicester Forest, to see the diversion of hunting, or rather the trailing of a cat before a pack of hounds : a custom, perhaps originating out of a claim to the royalty of the forest. Hither, on a fair day, resorted the young and old, and those of all denominations. In the greatest harmony the Spring was welcomed. The morning was spent in various amusements and athletic exercises, till a dead cat, about noon, was prepared by aniseed water, for commencing the mock-hunting of the hare. In about half-an-hour, after the cat had been trailed at the tail of a horse over the grounds in zig-zag directions, the hounds were directed to the spot where the cat had been trailed from. Here the hounds gave tongue in glorious concert. The people from the various eminences, who had placed themselves to behold the sight, with shouts of rapture gave applause ; the horsemen, dashing after the hounds through foul passages and over fences, were emulous for taking the lead of their fellows. It was a scene, upon the whole of joy, the governing and the governed in the habits of freedom enjoying together an innocent and recreating amusement, serving to unite them in bonds of mutual friendship, rather than to embitter their days with discord and disunion. As the cat had been trailed to the mayor's door, through some of the principal streets, consequently the dogs and horsemen followed.

---

* On Black Annis' Bower. See "Caves." Ed.

After the hunt was over, the mayor gave a handsome treat to his EASTER. friends ; in this manner the day ended." *

(This description is by an eye-witness of this old municipal custom, which' began to fall into disuse about the year 1767, although traces of it lingered within recent years in an annual holiday or fair held on the Danes' Hills and the Fosse Road on Easter Monday.

The first mention of the Easter hunting on the Danes' Hills in the Town Records occurs in the year 1668, but it was then an ancient custom, and it is so described; there are records of a similar hunt having taken place elsewhere more than a century earlier. Thus, in the Chamberlain's account for the year 1574 there is an item of 12*d.* "given to the hare-finders at Whetston Court," † and from this and other notices it appears that the hunting was originally, as might be expected, that of a real hare.

See " The Easter Hare " in " Folk-Lore," vol. iii.,

p. 441.   Ed.)

Easter Monday.—" The Dane-hill fair was crowded with visitors, principally young people of the working classes, and the fields beyond the spot where the fair is held were also thronged with merry-makers."

Leicester Chronicle, April 2, 1842.

This was called Black Monday.

1563.   P^d to the ringers on Black Monday . . xij^d.

Churchwarden's accounts of St. Martin's, Leicester.

From Mr. W. Kelly.

Hallaton " Hare Pie Scramble and Bottle Kicking."‡—In his notes

---

* Throsby's "History of Leicester."   Kelly's " Notices of Leicester, 1865," p. 168.   See North's "Chronicle of St. Martin's, 1866," p. 158.   Nichols, i., 449, note.   Ed.

† Kelly's " Notices of Leicester," pp. 173, 206, 278.   Shakespeare's " Much Ado About Nothing," Act i., Scene i.

‡ Hallaton-Hallowed or Holy Town.   Nichols, ii., 593 ; iii., 535.   Ed.

EASTER.   last week our correspondent "Inkling" briefly alluded to a singular Easter custom in a Leicestershire village. We are now enabled to give particulars from the pen of an eye witness. Our correspondent says:—" Before giving an account of the curious custom at Hallaton, a few words may be of interest respecting this small old-world town, which is situate on the eastern border of the shire, and possesses an antique cross and market square. Although its market has long been defunct, Hallaton still retains its two large ancient fairs, one held on Holy Thursday, and one on the third Thursday after. These were formerly of much greater importance, and the ale sold on fair days was a noted article in the district; for the convenience of the numerous people who attended, it was sold by any householder who chose to do so. Each seller simply puts up a bough in front of his house, and the houses so marked were called 'bough houses'—hence the saying, 'Good wine needs no bush.' The Sunday before the fair was called 'broaching Sunday,' or the Sunday for tasting the taps of the several 'bough houses.' That the place and surroundings are of great antiquity may be noted by the most casual observer, as about half-a-mile west is an encampment called 'The Castle Hill,' a lofty conical mound, of nearly 120 feet in height, with a circular entrenchment of about 200 yards; branching out from which, to the W., is a square plot of ground, encompassed with banks and ditches; and to the N.E. is a small square entrenchment connected with the outer fosse. To the S.W. of this is another encampment of about two acres. These earthworks are probably of British origin, with additions by later races of Roman, Saxon, Dane, and Norman, and are distinct from the celebrated 'Hare Pie Bank,' another historic earthwork. Doubtless the three manors the parish is in, and named respectively, 'Peveril,' 'Bardolph,' and 'Hackluyt,' are after names of their ancient owners. The church, recently restored by the munificence of the Peake family, is one of the finest and most interesting in the county, and forms a beautiful feature in the landscape. During the restoration, a fine crypt (until then unknown) was discovered under the east end of the north aisle, containing a large quantity of skulls similar to but smaller than the one at Rothwell. Standing upright beneath the chancel window are some fine sculptured stone coffin-lids in good preservation, with crosses carved upon them—evidently once belonging to ecclesiastics of the pre-Reformation period. The north porch contains a singularly large rough carved stone, doubtless older than the church itself, apparently of 'St. George and the Dragon,' built into the wall, which is of great interest to antiquarians. In the interior of the church are numerous memorials of old families, many of whose names are now no more known in the district. The origin of the custom associated with 'Hare Pie Bank' is lost in the mists of antiquity, and may be a relic of mediæval times, similar to the old 'Whipping Toms' in Leicester, put down in 1847. At all events, at a remote period, a piece of land was bequeathed to the rector conditionally that he and his successors provided annually 'Two hare pies, a quantity of ale, and two dozen penny loaves, to be scrambled for on each succeeding Easter Monday at the rising ground, called Hare Pie Bank,' about a quarter of a mile south of the village. This land, before the enclosure, was called 'Hare-cropleys,' and at the time of dividing the fields, in 1771, another piece of land was allotted to the rector in place of the 'Leys.' Of course, hares being 'out of season' at this time of the year, pies of mutton, veal, and bacon are substituted. (This year the loaves were dispensed with, an equivalent being given to the aged poor.) A benevolent rector of the last century made an effort to have the funds applied to a better use, but the village wags were equal to the occasion, and raised the cry and chalked on his walls and doors, as well as on the church, 'No pie, no parson, and a job for the glazier'; and again, in 1878, when the railway was in course of construction, parish meetings were held, to consider the desirability of taking the money and appropriating it to sports of other kinds, and more in character with the tastes of the age; many of the inhabitants, however, wishing to retain the old custom, the proposal fell through. As may well be imagined,

Easter Monday is the great carnival of the year, and eagerly looked forward to by the youths and natives of the place, as well as by the surrounding villagers. This year the two benefit societies, as usual, held their anniversary, one at the 'Royal Oak' and the other at the 'Fox Inn,' and to enliven the proceedings each engaged a band of musicians to accompany the members in processional order to the parish church, for the 'club sermon,' after which each society proceeded to their respective inns, where a substantial dinner was provided. About three p.m. a selected deputation called at the rectory for the provided 'pies and beer,' which upon being taken to the 'Fox Inn,' a procession was organised in the following order :—:

"Two men abreast, carrying two sacks with the pies cut up.

"Three men abreast, carrying aloft a bottle each; two of these bottles, filled with beer; are ordinary field wood bottles, but without the usual mouth, and are iron-hooped all over, with just a hole left for drinking from; the third is a 'dummy.'

"Occasionally, when it can be procured, as was the case in 1885, a hare, in sitting posture, mounted on top of a pole.

"Band of music.

"Procession, which, as may well be imagined, increases greatly in number as it approaches the 'Hare Pie Bank,' where, on arrival, the pies cut up are pitched out of the sack and scrambled for.

"Until this year a man followed the band with a basket containing the penny loaves, which were broken up and thrown about indiscriminately as he went along. On Monday, when the procession neared the bank, the band struck up 'See the conquering hero comes,' and, on reaching the bank, the hare-pies were scrambled for by the spectators, who amused themselves by throwing the contents at each other. Then commenced in earnest the business of the day—the well-known 'Hallaton bottle-kicking.' One of the large bottles containing ale—both of which are of wood strongly iron-hooped—was thrown into the circular hollow on the mound, when the 'Medbourne men,' or other villagers who cared to join, tried to wrest the bottle from the Hallatonians' grasp. Talk of a football scrimmage! It was nothing to this. First one side then the other prevailed, the object of the Hallatonians being to kick or get the bottle, by hook or by crook, to their boundary line over the brook adjoining the village. As each side was rough and determined some fierce struggles ensued, especially when the surging mass of villagers reached a post-and-rail fence, which, giving way, precipitated the lot heels over head into the highway. Here followed the roughest part of the contest, as 'the strangers' nearly succeeded in getting the bottle over the adjoining fence, which, if accomplished, would have enabled them to work the much-prized object to the Medbourne boundary. However, they were unsuccessful, as the prize was again got on the bank, and after a scene of good-humoured disorder that baffles description was, after half-an-hour's tussle, got on to the ground sloping to the brook, and after being conveyed over two or three fences and ditches, was, amid the loud applause of the natives, safely got over the water—which was not the case with some of the combatants, who landed *in* the water. The victors of course claimed the contents. Next came 'the dummy,' which if anything was contested for with even keener zest, for the Hallaton people boast that this has never yet got beyond their grasp, and they are not a little proud of their possession, which they do not at present seem at all likely to lose. The third bottle was then taken in triumph to the Market-cross, and its contents drunk with 'due honours.' The bottles for the occasion are carefully kept from year to year, and those now in use have done duty for more than thirty years. The present 'bottle holder' is Mr. Omar Neale, who takes a great interest in seeing the old custom perpetuated (which many might think more honoured in the breach than in the observance), and brightens up with animation when recounting the various incidents of note that have occurred during his stewardship."

Mr. Thomas Spencer, *Leicester Journal*, April 22, 1892.

EASTER.

[*See* Nichols, II., 600 ; and see " The Easter Hare " in " Folk-Lore," vol. iii., p. 441. Ed.] *See also* under " Caves."

Easter Shilling.—" At the Easter Court at Leicester " (of the Honour of Winton, originally part of the Honour of Leicester) " according to ancient custom a shilling is brought into the court-room in a sack-bag across a cowl-staff borne on two men's shoulders, when a scuffle ensues, and the man who can first get possession of the bag has the shilling."

Nichols, I., 624.

HOLY THURSDAY.

Hallaton Holy Thursday Fair.—Next day, being what is termed the holy day fair, was enlivened by a procession of Odd Fellows, who, after hearing a sermon at the Church, paraded the village preceded by an excellent band of music.

Leicester Chronicle, May 14, 1842.

Holy Thursday Fair at Loughborough.—As to Holy Thursday fair, commonly so called, it is no fair by grant or proclamation, but only a customary resort of young people to Loughborough on that particular day, for their pleasure and amusement.

Nichols, III., 890.

WHITSUN-TIDE.

Sports.—At Burrow Hill, the races, held in much later times on the level ground within the earthworks at the top, drew together annually a large concourse of people. Leland thus describes these sports : " To these Borowe hills every year on Monday after White Sunday, com people of the country there-abouts, and shoote, runne, wrestle, dance, and use other feats of like exercise."

" By-gone Leicestershire," p. 123.

[*See* Nichols, III., 531. Ed.]

Whit Monday Procession.—*Oblation of Gloves.*—" A solemn pro-cession took place annually, on Whit Monday, from the Church of

St. Mary within the Castle to St. Margaret's without the walls of WHITSUN-
TIDE. the town. . . . . where oblations were made at the high altar. These consisted, in part, of two pairs of gloves; one pair said to be for God, and the other for St. Thomas of India."

> " Notices Illustrative of the Drama and other Popular
> Amusements chiefly in the 16th and 17th Cen-
> turies, incidentally illustrating Shakespeare and
> his Contemporaries; extracted from the Cham-
> berlains' Accounts and other Manuscripts of the
> Borough of Leicester." With an Introduction
> and Notes by William Kelly. (London: John
> Russell Smith, Soho Square, 1865), pp. 7, 8.
> [See also Nichols, I., 305, 562 n, 569. Ed.]

Lord of Misrule at Melton.—There is among the Melton manuscripts, "A Reckoning and Accompt" of Robert Odam, junior,
who, as Lord of Misrule of Melton, at Whitsuntide, 1563 charges
his accompt with:—

Itm. a pottell of wyne to Kettleby to Mr. Patts - - - - -	viijd.
Itm. for spyce for the cakes - - -	xxid.
Itm. to the iiij footemen - - -	viijs.
Itm. to the ij buttlers - - -	xxd.

The Lord of Misrule, with his company, visited Mr. Pate,
to gather his " Devocyn for the repaving and mending the
highewayes."

> "Transactions of the Leicestershire Architectural
> and Archaeological Societies," vol. iv., page 264.
> *See also* under "Folk Drama."

Whitsuntide Procession at Hinckley.—A fair used to be held on
Whitsun Monday at Hinckley, when the millers from various
parts of the country walked in procession, dressed in ribbons,
with what they called the "king of the millers" at their head.
A writer (in 1785 *) quoted in Thistleton Dyer's "British

* This is an error for 1787. Ed.

Popular Customs," describing one of those fairs, says: "To the old ceremony of riding millers, many improvements were made upon a more extensive and significant plan : several personages were introduced that bore allusions to the manufacture, and were connected with the place. Old Hugo Baron de Greutemaisuel, who made his first appearance in 1786 (*sic.*), armed in light and easy pasteboard armour, was this second time armed cap-a-pie in heavy sinker plate, with pike and shield, on the latter the arms of the town. The representative Baron of Hinckley had the satisfaction of being accompanied by his lady, the Baroness Adeliza, habited in the true antique style, with steeple-hat, ruff-points, mantle, &c., all in suitable colours ; each riding on nimble white steeds properly caparisoned ; they were preceded by the town banner, and two red streamers embroidered with their respective names. Several bands of music gave cheerful spirit to the pageant, but more particularly the militia band from Leicester. The framework knitters, wool-combers, butchers, carpenters, &c., had each their plays, and rode in companies, bearing devices or allusions to their several trades. Two characters, well represented and supported, were Bishop Blaise and his chaplain, who figured at the head of the wool-combers. In their train appeared a pretty innocent pair, a gentle shepherd and shepherdess ; the latter carrying a lamb, the emblem of her little self more than of the trade." " Some other little folks, well dressed," proceeds the old narrative, " were mounted on ponies, holding instruments, the marks of their father's business, and ornamented with ribbons of all colours waving in the air." T. B. T.

" Leicestershire Notes and Queries," vol. i., p. 33.

(This account is quoted verbally from Dyer's " British Popular Customs " (Bohn), p. 285.)

See also Nichols' "History of Hinckley," 1813, p. 678 ; Nichols' "Leicestershire," IV., 674, 676-678. Ed.

Robin Hood's Play.—*See* under "Folk-Drama."

Wymondham.—There is a Singing Feast held here on every WHITSUN-
TIDE. Monday in Whitsun-week.

Nichols, II., 406.

The Ratby Meadow.—In the parish of Ratby there is a meadow adjoining the road from Market Bosworth to Leicester. Before the fields were enclosed this meadow belonged to several occupiers of land in the parish of Ratby. The custom was to mow their several allotments on a certain day called "the meadow-morning," as was also the custom in several other parts of the county, particularly at Nailston, Desford, Stanton-under-Bardon, &c. When the labour of the day was over, the remaining part was spent with music and dancing on a small eminence in one part of the meadow. It happened in the latter part of the reign of Edward III., or beginning of the reign of Richard II., that John of Gaunt, Duke of Lancaster and Earl of Leicester, fourth son of Edward III., passed by the meadow on his way to Leicester, where he kept his Court, attended by only one servant, on the day of the meadow-morning. Observing mirth and festivity, he alighted from his horse, and asked the cause of diversion. They told him they had been mowing the meadow which was called *Ramsdale*, according to their annual custom. Having joined with them in their diversions, he was so well pleased with their innocent pastimes that when he took his leave he told them if they would meet him at Leicester, at such a time and place as he appointed, he would give to each of them a ewe to their ram, also a wether whose grassy fleece should annually, when sold, make them a splendid repast. There was a consultation immediately held; some said it was a joke, others that they were determined to know the truth of the matter. Accordingly, about fifteen persons set out for Leicester, and went to the appointed place, where they found the Duke, who informed them that if they would keep the following "articles" he would give to each of them a piece or parcel of land situated in a meadow, in the parish of Enderby, in the said county of Leicester, adjoining the River Soar, and near

2 4

unto an ancient burying-ground called St. John's Churchyard, containing by measure half-an-acre, which was to be called " The Ewes," for each man's private use; also another small piece for every person to be called "The Boots," about five yards wide and fifty or sixty yards long; and he would likewise give them a piece or parcel of land for their general use, to be called " The Wether," containing about two acres, adjoining the River Soar (which is said in a rainy season " to wash the wether's breech "): the grass crop to be sold annually on Whit Monday at Enderby to the best bidder. The proceeds (of late years amounting to £4 or upwards) to defray the expense of the annual feast on Whit Monday.

Articles:

That there shall be two persons chosen annually by a majority, to be called caterers, who shall on every Whit Monday go to Leicester, to what inn they shall think proper, when a calf's head shall be provided for their breakfast; and when the bones are picked clean, they are to be put into a dish and served up with the dinner. Likewise, the innkeeper is to provide two large rich pies for the caterers to take home, that their families may partake of some of their festivities. Likewise, there shall be provided for every person a short silk lace, tagged at both ends with silver, being equipped with which they shall all proceed to Enderby, and sell the grass of the Wether to the best bidder; from thence shall go to the meadow and all dismount, and each person shall take a small piece of grass from the before mentioned Wether and tie it round with their tagged lace, and wear it in their hats, and ride in procession to the High Cross in Leicester, and there throw them among the populace; from thence proceed to their inn, and go in procession to St. Mary's Church, when a sermon shall be preached for the benefit of an hospital founded by Henry, Earl of Lancaster. When service is over, a deed shall be read over by the clergyman concerning the above gift, and the church shall be stuck with flowers. When the ceremony is over, they are to return to to their inn to dinner, and close the day with mirth and festivity.

Throsby's "History of Leicester," 1790, vol. ii., p. 84.

W. H. Y., in " Leicestershire Notes and Queries," after quoting
the above account says, " The ceremonies, though still maintained,
have varied in detail in the course of years, but the following
account, given to the writer by one of this year's merry-makers,
will show that the spirit of the thing still survives :—

" The caterer orders lunch at an inn at Enderby at 11 a.m., consisting of flat, stilton, and cream cheese, butter, various cakes,
cucumber, raddish, onions, watercress, etc., with plenty of home-
brewed ales, which makes a hearty meal ; the table is nicely
decorated with flowers. He then proceeds to sell the grass on the
Wether, usually at about one p.m. He then, with the riders,
eighteen in number, proceeds to an inn at Leicester, where
dinner has been previously ordered, together with a lunch for ten
inmates of Trinity Hospital, which latter must consist of calf's
head, bacon, etc., and one quart of ale each. When the riders
arrive at the inn, the custom is to drink from a quart of ale before
alighting, the oldest of the hospitallers having thrown the bones
of the calf's head under the horse of the first to arrive. The
riders are then shown to the dining-room, which is tastefully
decorated—this year it was at the Golden Lion, High Cross St.—
and an ample meal is served, consisting of several courses. Dinner
concluded, two bottles of brandy are brought, and all standing
drink 'To the immortal memory of John o' Gaunt.' The table
is then spread with dessert, and the bill having been called for, to
see how far the money will hold out, the evening is spent in
conviviality."

" Leicestershire Notes and Queries," i., pp. 224-6.

In accordance with the Charter of John o'Gaunt, the annual
sale of the "keep" on that portion of the Ratby Meadows
known as "The Wether" (about two acres) took place at the
Nag's Head, at Enderby, on Whit Monday, Mr. J. Fossell, of
Leicester, acting as "caterer." As usual a capital lunch was

served, there being about 30 persons present. The ancient custom of passing a penny round the table during the bidding was followed, and for some time "business." was fairly brisk. Eventually "The Wether" was bought by Mr. Robt. Palmer for £7 18s., a price considerably higher than has been realised for a number of years. A somewhat animated discussion, which lasted about two hours, ensued as to the right of spending on that day the proceeds of the sale, save the usual expenses, in providing a dinner for 18 persons, a proceeding which all present contended, with the exception of the "caterer," ought to be carried out. Mr. Fossell maintained that in the absence of certain "owners" of shares in the Ratby Meadows he had no legal right to expend the balance of upwards of £6 in providing a dinner that day, and under the circumstances he urged them to postpone the dinner to some future occasion. Those present however, contended that to hold the dinner on any other day would be going against the charter. Throsby's "History of Leicestershire" was produced, and the reading of the portion relating to the charter in question appeared to give an impetus to the discussion, in the course of which it was stated that "The Wether" had not been properly sold for the last two years, and the "caterer" was questioned as to the income and expenditure in connection with the land for the two years named. Mr. Fossell replied that there were no accounts to be found in the book, but Mr. Cox, who held several shares in the Ratby Meadows, had informed him that the proceeds from the land during the last two years had been expended in improvements. ("Shame, shame," and voices, "What, for one day's work on the land?") A parishioner: What improvements have been made? Mr. Fossell: There are none mentioned in the book. (Laughter.) After a good deal more discussion, the purchaser of "The Wether" emphatically declared that he would not pay the money until he knew whether it would be spent on that day or not. The "caterer," however, continued to calmly refuse to accede to the wishes of the gathering, but eventually the money was paid on the understanding that Mr. Fossell, after deducting the usual expenses from the total proceeds, should hand over the balance to the "caterer" for next year (Mr. W. Herbert), who was present, and thus free himself of all responsibility connected with the expending of the remainder of the money, this proposition of Mr. Fossell's being greeted with enthusiastic cheers. The proposition was carried out, Mr. Fossell was duly thanked, and in the evening a party partook of a capital dinner at the Blue Boar Hotel, Leicester. As far as we know, however, there was no riding through the brook, which used to be done in olden times prior to partaking of the dinner.

Leicester Daily Post, May 16, 1894.

[*See* Nichols, IV., 880-882. Ed.]

WHITSUN-
TIDE.

The time-honoured custom of perambulating the parish of St. Mary took place on Thursday, and, favoured by fine weather, the holiday proved in every way a successful and enjoyable one. The "beating of the bounds," as it is called, is an institution that has been observed in connection with St. Mary's from time immemorial. Indeed, it is well recognised as a parish holiday, and in modern times at any rate has consisted for the most part in feasting and merry-making, though it is quite conceivable that in more ancient and less civilised days the re-marking of a parish boundary would result in bitter strife and inter-parochial jealousy. It is only fair to say, perhaps, that there is no particular ground for such an assumption, except that in order to carry out the function properly even in these degenerate days it requires a regiment of small boys armed with penny canes. The custom, singularly enough, is not kept up annually, but every three years, and there can be no doubt that on the part of the youngsters it is eagerly looked forward to. The arrangements on this occasion were ably carried out by a small committee, consisting of Mr.

BEATING
THE
BOUNDS.

2 4 *

William Earp (assistant overseer), Mr. George Hall, and Mr. Joseph Berridge, under the direction of the overseers, Messrs. J. B. Taylor, E. Pickard, W. Gimson, jun., and John Spencer. Another gentleman who took an active interest in the ceremony was Mr. W. Sheen, now in his 87th year, and who has attended every perambulation of the parish for the last sixty years or more. The start was made from St. Mary's Schools, Castle Street, where something like 250 boys assembled, these consisting of the scholars from St. Mary's and Trinity Church Schools, and a number selected from the three Board schools in the parish. The boys, who wore red badges, were marshalled into procession by Mr. Earp, that genial and indefatigable official acting as guide and general cicerone throughout the perambulation. Accompanied by the vicar (Rev. H. W. Orford) and other gentlemen associated with the parish, the procession moved off at a quarter to nine, the line of route for the first mile or so being by way of Bath Lane, Applegate Street, Harvey Lane, Redcross Street, Friar Lane, Millstone Lane, Oxford Street, the Newarkes, and Wellington Street, into New Walk. The most exciting incident so far was an attack with a crutch on the part of an exasperated lady parishioner in retaliation for the alleged breaking of a window. The boundary line passes through a house between New Walk and Wellington Street, and in spite of such sentiment as one hears about the Englishman's home being his castle, the "beaters" invaded the precincts of the domicile in question in apparently the most summary fashion, though it was remarked that both doors were wide open, as if the visitors were expected. Some difficulty was experienced in finding the boundary stone near the top of New Walk, but after a painstaking search it was unearthed amid exultant cheers, and the war-paint having been brought into requisition, the beaters again moved on.

The triennial perambulation dinner took place in the evening at the Golden Lion Hotel, Highcross Street, the vicar, Rev. H. W. Orford, presiding.

Leicester Daily Post, May 4, 1894.

In former years upon the arrival of the procession at Redhill, close near the Narborough Road, a homily was read by the vicar in a part of the field surrounded by a bank of earth, after which a hole was dug and any newly-appointed parish officer was seized, turned topsy-turvy, and his head placed in the hole, whilst his "latter end" was saluted with the shovel. He was expected to pay 5s. for being thus made free. I recollect one of the curates being thus dealt with. An adjournment then took place to a marquee, where lunch was provided for all comers, and buns and ale were distributed to the children. Various sports, such as racing, bobbing for apples in buckets of water, &c., then took place, after which the perambulation was resumed. The expenses were formerly paid out of the church rates.

BEATING THE BOUNDS.

From Mr. W. Kelly.

See also post, p. 93.

About Croft Hill are some little eminences called *Shepherds' Tables*. It was the custom, in former times, for shepherds to have a day of festivity at certain seasons of the year at these kind of summits, which were cast up for the purpose. Neatherds, at this day, have not wholly laid aside the old custom of carousing on Old May-Day, in turning the cows to the common pasture.

MAY DAY.

Nichols' "History of Leicestershire," IV., part ii., "Sparkenhoe Hundred," pp. 583, 584.

The First of May has been an occasion for gladness and rejoicing since earliest times. Maplewell (May-pole-well), near Woodhouse, is said to be the spot where the forest celebrations of this festival took place. In the "Tablette Book" of Lady Mary Keyes (a sister of Lady Jane Grey), a quaint description is given of May-Day at Bradgate in the 16th century: "Then, when the merrie May Pole and alle the painted Morris-dancers, withe Tabor and Pipe, beganne their spritelie anticks on our butiful grene laune.

MAY DAY. afore that we idel leetel Bodyes had left owre warme Bedds,
woulde goode Mistress Bridget, the Tire-woman whom our Lady
Mother alwaies commanded to do owre Biddings, com and telle us
of the merrie men a-dancing on the Grene." On May morning
the milkmaids would repair to the fields with pails bedecked with
flowers. In some villages, arches of evergreen were erected, in
others a large Maypole was carried round (occasionally on Whit
Monday), and ancient doggrel shouted in chorus :—

> " Riggany, raggany,
> Ten pin flaggany ;
> Eighteen pole."

The first two lines of this apparently meaningless jingle were said
very rapidly, the third with the syllables long drawn out.

" Bygone Leicestershire," p. 122.

May-Day at Ashby-de-la-Zouch.—Bands of girls, some hailing
from the adjacent villages, perambulated the town on Tuesday,
bearing miniature maypoles tastefully decorated with flowers.

Leicester Daily Post, Wednesday, May 2nd, 1894.

May-poles.—In the month of May, 1603, a collision occurred
between the populace and the authorities of Leicester, on account
of the setting up of a maypole in the South-gate.

For an account of this and other disturbances of the
same kind, *see* Kelly's " Notices," pp. 100-111.

Maypoles, &c.—A regulation made by the Corporation (of
Leicester) on the 20th of November, 5th Edward VI., entitled
" An Acte for Cuttynge of Bowes," provided that " if there be
any man, woman, or child taken or known to have broken or cut
down in the summer time or any other time, any oak-boughs,
hawthorn-boughs, or any other boughs, *to set at their doors or
windows*, out of any close garden or orchard about this town of
Leicester, or within the liberties of the same, to forfeit for every

time taken or proved with such default xij^{d.} and their bodies to   **MAY.**
prison, there to remain during Mr. Mayor's will and pleasure."

Kelly's "Notices," p. 72, quoting "Town Book of
Acts," p. 36.

See also under "Tree and Plant Superstitions." [Maypoles.]

29th May.—"Oak-apple Day" is still generally observed throughout the county by the wearing of oak-apples and oak-leaves.
Those who have none are liable to be stung with nettles by those
who have them. [Ed.]

On the 29th of May (at Hinckley) the ringers (in addition to
ringing merry peals) used to place large boughs of oak over the
doors of the houses occupied by the principal inhabitants, and
always fixed a large bough on the battlements of the church.
This custom is now discontinued.

North's "Church Bells of Leicestershire," p. 187.

Beating the Bounds.—There is an annual perambulation (at
Shepeshed) on Ascension Day.

Nichols, III., 1018.

"Processioning" time at Ashby Wolds, the 29th of May.

"Transactions of the Leicestershire Architectural
and Archaeological Societies," vol. i., p. 33.

See also ante, p. 89.

Morris-Dancers.—"On Plow Monday I have taken notice of   **PLOUGH**
an annual display of Morris-dancers at Claybrook, who come   **MONDAY.**
from the neighbouring villages of Sapcote and Sharnford."

"The History and Antiquities of Claybrook, in the
County of Leicester," by the Rev. A. Macaulay,
M.A. (London: printed for the Author by
J. Nichols: MDCCXCI.), page 128.
Brand's "Antiquities," i., 509.
Dyer's "British Popular Customs" (Bohn), p. 40.

Plough Monday.—On Plough Monday it was the custom for

PLOUGH
MONDAY.

some of the villagers to dress in grotesque masquerade, and perform morris-dances before all the houses where they were likely to get money or drink. Sometimes they were accompanied by a gang of lads with ruddled faces, half-hidden under paper masks, who dragged a plough, but this was unusual. Some of the performers, generally four, had on white women's dresses and tall hats. One of these was called Maid Marian. Of the other performers one was the fool, who always carried the money-box, and generally a bladder with peas in it on a string at the end of a stick, with which he laid lustily about him. Another was Beelzebub, in a dress made up of narrow strips of flannel, cloth, &c., with the ends hanging loose—yellow, red, black, and white being the predominant colours The rest were simply grotesques. The dance they performed was merely a travesty of a quadrille, with *ad. lib.* stamping and shuffling of feet. On one occasion, when I was very little, the fool came up and asked me to "remember the fool;" adding, in case I might not have recognised him through his disguise, "I'm Curly." "Yes," I said, "I see you are; and I shall remember you, Curly, as long as I live." "Tell 'im the *bullocks* is thirsty an' wants some beer," said one of the performers; "a' doon't knoo what yo mane." From that Plough-Monday I date my knowledge of what "remembrance" means in the mouth of a son of the soil.

Evans, p. 215.

[*See* Nichols, IV., 896 (Sapcote), and Mary Kirby's "Leaflets from my Life," London, 1887, for Plough Monday at Thurcaston in 1839. Ed.]

MID-
SUMMER.

See under "Tree and Plant Superstitions" [Hempseed], and under "Magic and Divination."

See "Wakes."

ALL
SAINTS'
DAY.

The children here (Godeby) have regularly a bonfire on All Saints' Day.

Nichols, II., 196.

Hallaton.—Barring-out.—Thirty years ago there was a curious **ST. ANDREW'S DAY.** custom allowed here (at Hallaton) on St. Andrew's Day. The children locked the master out of the belfry, and jangled the bells. This custom was discontinued upon the death of the then aged master..

North's "Church Bells of Leicestershire," p. 183.

Gooding.—"Going a-gooding" is going round from house to **ST. CLEMENT'S DAY.** house collecting money, fruit, vegetables, &c., as on St. Clement's Day. At Market Bosworth the song sung on St. Clement's Day by the boys who go gooding runs thus :—

> "St. Clement's, St. Clement's, St. Clement's is here ;
> Apples and pears are very good cheer ;
> One for St. Peter, and one for St. Paul,
> And three for Him who made us all.
> Up with the kettle and down with the pan !
> Give us some apples and we will be gone !" Evans, p. 162.

Going a-gowding.—Has this any connection with a custom which lingered till within recent years in some of the villages of giving doles on the morning after the Feast Sunday ? At Frisby-on-the-Wreke a group of poor people used to go from house to house receiving a dole of milk from each. Frisby Church is dedicated to St. Thomas à Becket, and the place was a great stronghold of Romanism. Had the dole anything to do with the vigil in the church the night before, and was this a way of paying the beadsmen ?

From Miss H. Ellis.

[*See* Northall, 222 and 228. Ed.]

This day was formerly celebrated in Rutlandshire by fowlers **ST. TIBBA'S DAY.** and falconers, who regarded the saint as their peculiar patroness. Camden mentions the town of Ryhall as particularly addicted to this superstitious observance, and the passage, which is strongly expressed, was ordered to be expunged from his "Britannia" by the "Index Expurgationis," printed at Madrid in 1612 by Louis Sanchez.

"Med. Ævi. Kalend." i., p. 82.   Quoted in Dyer's
"British Popular Customs" (Bohn), p. 438.

Rihall, ubi cum majores nostros ita fascinasset superstitio, ut leorum multitudine Deum verum propemodum sustulisset, Tibba minorum gentium diva, quasi Diana ab aucupibus utique rei accipitrariæ præses colebatur.

> Camden, "Britannia," 8vo. Lond. edit. 1590, p. 419.
> [See also Blore's "History of Rutland," p. 59. Ed.]
> See also under "Holy Wells."

CHRIST-
MAS.

Wassailing.—"Old John Payne and his wife, natives of this parish, are well known from having perambulated the hundred of Guthlaxton many years, during the season of Christmas, with a fine gew-gaw which they call a *wassail*, and which they exhibit from house to house with the accompaniment of a duet. I apprehend that the practice of wassailing will die with this aged pair."

> Macaulay's "Claybrook," p. 131.
> Quoted in Brand's "Popular Antiquities of Great Britain" (Bohn), 1890, i., p. 6.

INNO-
CENT'S
DAY.

Playing in Church.—When living in the parish of Exton, Rutland, some 15 years ago, I was told by an old lady that in her girlhood, in the very early years of this century, it was the custom for children to be allowed to play in the church on "Innocents' Day": At that time the grandfather of the Bishop of Gloucester and Bristol was vicar of Exton. It would be, I suppose, a survival of a Miracle Play or the Boy Bishop.

> "Leicestershire Notes and Queries," i., 293.

MICHAEL-
MAS DAY.

See under "Local Customs."   [High Cross Fair.]

WAKES.

"At this time" (Circa 1788) "every village had its wake, and the lower orders were comparatively in a state of ease and plenty. Then every place was proud of its maypole and spacious green, kept for sports and pastimes. . . . The maypole with its pastimes, and the games of singlestick and wrestling have now disappeared. These were the sports of the ruder part WAKES. of the peasantry."

Gardiner's "Music and Friends," i., pp. 43, 44.

Wake.—The wake was originally a religious festival, and in the country it still retains its religious character to a greater extent than is done in most towns. . . . . This is almost the only custom that has not fallen into disuse. . . . . Musicians and morris-dancers used to go round the country villages at certain seasons. Claybrooke and some other neighbouring villages were noted for those customs, which are now nearly all gone. The last to go seems to be the observance of "Plough Monday" but even this is very much on the wane and cannot survive much longer.

Rev. C. Holme, "History of Guthlaxton Deaneries
and adjacent parishes," Rugby, 1891, p. 38.

Wake at the Oaks Chapel.—The inhabitants of the forest, to commemorate the foundation of the first Forest Church, and struck, perhaps, by the coincidence of its being consecrated on what is now called "Waterloo-Day," attempted for some years to keep up a wake on the anniversary; the custom, however, soon fell into disuse.

"History and Antiquities of Charnwood Forest."
T. R. Potter, 1842, p. 39.

Wake at Nanpantan.—The Annual Wake, now kept on Nanpantan, but formerly kept on Beacon, the origin of which is lost in obscurity, may be a remnant of one of these (Druidical) festivals.

"History and Antiquities of Charnwood Forest,"
T. R. Potter, 1842, p. 45 (note).

Wakes.—"There is a wake the Sunday next after St. Peter, to whom the church is dedicated. . . . . The people of this neighbourhood are much attached to the celebration of wakes; and on the annual return of those festivals, the cousins assemble from all quarters, fill the church on Sunday, and celebrate Monday with feasting, with musick, and with dancing."

> Macaulay's " Claybrook," 1791, pp. 93, 128.
> Quoted in Brand's "Popular Antiquities" (Bohn), vol. ii., p. 12.
> Nichols, IV., 131.

The annual wake or feast held at Shepeshed is on the Sunday next after old Midsummer Day.

> Nichols, III., 1018.

The wake (at Whitwick) is on the Sunday after Midsummer Day.

> Nichols, III., 1120.

Feast—a "wake," an annual gathering or small fair held in villages, hamlets, &c. It is generally supposed that the *feast* commemorates the day of the saint to whom the parish church is dedicated; and this is sometimes the case, though not in the majority of instances. Nearly all the *feasts* take place in the summer and autumn, and are generally so arranged that the *feast* of one village does not clash with the *feast* of any other in the neighbourhood.

> Evans' " Leicestershire Words and Phrases," ed. 1881, p. 147.

See also under " Local Customs." [Haystrewing.]

The Reeve Meadow and Meadow-mowing at Desford.—In the manor of Desford there are eighteen Reeve-houses, the owners of which have the "Reeve Meadow" annually in succession, and should any one person own more than one such house, he has the field in his turn for each. Possession of the field is taken by the one succeeding to it on the first of January each year (who at once puts lock and key thereon). The Reeve for the year has the produce thereof, either for his own use or for sale, and in addition to finding the dinner for the Court Baron the following year, and paying £2 to the steward thereat, has to provide a certain sum (about fifty shillings) for prizes at the "Meadow-mowing," as it is called, which takes place the week after the hay is carried, and consists of wrestling, running, and other games. Should a Reeve-house be wholly pulled down, it loses its rights, so that when at any time one requires rebuilding, it is usual to leave a chimney or some portion of the building standing.

The Meadow-mowing was, according to Throsby and Nichols, a custom in the olden time in several parts of the country, and was the occasion of much merriment, festivity, and games.—*Vide* "Notes and Queries," vol. i., p. 224, for details of the custom in vogue at Ratby.

REEVE MEADOW-MOWING.

" Leicestershire Notes and Queries," ii., p. 111..

The Riding of the George.—Our local historian, Throsby,[*] has doubtless not exaggerated in describing the "riding of the George" as the "grandest solemnity of the town," for it appears to have been celebrated by the whole of the inhabitants, from the highest to the lowest, as one of the greatest festivity and rejoicing, and naturally to have attracted numerous spectators from the surrounding villages.

RIDING OF THE GEORGE.

The day for the "riding" having been fixed (for it did not always take place on St. George's Day), the master of the Guild caused proclamation to be made at the High Cross, and elsewhere, of the time appointed, and, in all probability, special invitations were sent to the county magnates, for we find that not unfrequently the Earl of Huntingdon and others of the nobility and gentry of the neighbourhood attended, and were presented with wine, &c., by the mayor and corporation, who also officially joined the master and brethren of the Guild in the procession. Nor was this a mere matter of choice, but one alike of immemorial usage and compulsion; for an express order, or "Act" of Common Hall, made in 1467, and subsequently confirmed, enjoined all the inhabitants, on being warned or summoned, "to attend upon the n   or to ride against (*i.e.* to meet) the King, or for riding of the George, or any other

<hr/>

[*] " History of Leicester," p. 242.

thing that shall be to the pleasure of the mayor and worship for the town."

. . . . . We find, a quarter of a century later, that the riding of the George had, for some years, ceased to be celebrated. To enforce the performance of this ceremony for the future, it was ordered by the mayor and his brethren, at a Common Hall, held in November, 1523,* in the third mayoralty of Richard Reynolds, that whoever should thereafter be master of Saint George's Guild " should cause the George to be ridden, according to *the old ancient custom*, that is to say, between St. George's Day and Whit Sunday, unless there be reasonable cause " . . . . .

These particulars comprise the substance of all the information we are able to derive from the Borough Records respecting this ancient custom, with the exception of one suggestive entry in the Chamberlain's Account for 1536; and it will be seen they do not afford us the slightest insight into the nature of the ceremonies observed on the occasion, or whether any character, in addition to St. George, was represented in the pageant.

That the saint, however, was not the only figure in the procession of the Guild is clearly evinced by this single entry, which records that, in this instance, the chamberlains of the town, and not the brethren of the Guild, " paid for *dressing of the dragon*, 4s. ; " and it is probable that the other characters in the legend were also represented, as, fortunately, the records of another ancient city, which possessed a similar fraternity, enable us to decide with tolerable certainty on this point.

[Here follows an account of the " Riding of the George," at Norwich, extracted from Muskett's " Notices and Illustrations of the Costume, Processions, Pageantry, &c., formerly displayed by the Corporation of Norwich." See also *Edinburgh Review*, vol. lxxvii. (1843), p. 144.]

Kelly's " Notices of Leicester," pp. 45-49.

At Leicester, the " riding of the George " was one of the

---

* Not 1504, as stated in Mr. James Thompson's " History of Leicester."

principal solemnities of the town. The inhabitants were bound
to attend the mayor, or to "ride against the King," as it is expressed, or for "riding the George," or for any other thing to the
pleasure of the mayor, and worship of the town. St. George's
horse, harnessed, used to stand at the end of St. George's Chapel,
in St. Martin's Church, Leicester.

> Fosbroke's "Dictionary of Antiquities."
> Quoted in Dyer's "British Popular Customs"
> (Bohn), p. 198, also in "Leicestershire Notes
> and Queries," i., 112.
> Nichols, I., 376, 390, 391, 392, and 591.
> Cf also "Folk-Lore," vol. ii., 326-328. Ed.

Bull-Baiting.—The town books of Leicester contain numerous
references to this subject. It is stated in the Records that at a
meeting held at the Common Hall on the Thursday before the
Feast of Saints Simon and Jude,* the following order was
made : "That no butcher kill a bull to sell within the Town
before it is baited." If the regulation were disregarded, the
offender was liable to the forfeiture of the dead animal.

> Andrews' "Bygone England" (London, 1892), p. 170.

Elmesthorpe. From Richard Fowkes' "Extremesis," 1811 :—
Jan. 7. Plow Monday.—

> " The old custom of Plough Monday still prevails
> Like a great many more old popular tales.
> Plough bullocks dressed in ribbons, a gaudy show,
> In a long procession, shouting as they go."

Feb. 6.—I was this morning observing the old superstitious
making of crosses upon the malt after it was mashed in the mash-
tub. It is common almost everywhere amongst the women when
they brew, to make crosses to keep the witch out of the mash-tub
and that the ale may be fine.

---

* In 1467. [*See* Kelly, "Notices of Leicester," pp. 159 and 185. Nichols, I.,
375. Ed.]

March 14.—Easter Sunday.—" The sun dances on Easter Sunday in the morning."

May 11.—It hath been a custom time out of mind for children to scatter flowers before people's doors in towns on May-Day.

May 26.—Farmers and common people extremely ignorant and illiterate, even vulgar in the highest degree, and very great believers in old popular tales of ghosts, fairies, witches, and people and cattle being under an evil tongue ; nailing horse-shoe with nine holes on stable door, and keeping one always in the fire ; and a hundred more superstitious pranks.

June 21.—*Longest Day.*—Shearing our sheep. Such dainties at village sheep-shearing, till gaping boys and men have seen the bottom of the brown jug and copious horn—and a garland of flowers on the ram's neck to grace this rural day.

> " Transactions of the Leicestershire Architectural
> and Archaeological Societies," vol. iv., pp. 296
> and 297.

Church Ales.—See Nichols, I., 305.

Waits.—See Nichols, I., 397, 401, 402, 467.

(b) CEREMONIAL CUSTOMS.

It is unlucky to weigh children. If you do, they will probably die, and at any rate will not thrive.

When children first leave their mother's room, they must go *upstairs* before they go downstairs, otherwise they will never rise in the world.

> From Mr. J. D. Paul.
> Chambers' "Book of Days," vol. ii., p. 39.
> [Cf. Black, "Folk Medicine," p. 180.   Ed.]

A custom exists in the town of Leicester of rather a singular nature. The first time a new-born child pays a visit it is presented with an egg, a pound of salt, and a bundle of matches.

BIRTH CUSTOMS.

"Notes and Queries," vol. vii. (1853), p. 128.

Riding for the Bride-Cake, and other Wedding Customs.—A custom formerly prevailed in this parish and neighbourhood of "riding for the bride-cake," which took place when the bride was brought home to her new habitation. A pole was erected in the front of the house, three or four yards high, with the cake stuck upon the top of it; on the instant that the bride set out from her old habitation, a company of young men started off on horseback; and he who was fortunate enough to reach the pole first, and knock the cake down with his stick, had the honour of receiving it from the hands of a damsel on the point of a wooden sword; and with this trophy he returned in triumph to meet the bride and her attendants, who, upon their arrival in the village, were met by a party whose office it was to adorn their horses' heads with garlands, and to present the bride with a posey.

WEDDING CUSTOMS.

The last ceremony of this sort that took place in the parish of Claybrook was between sixty and seventy years ago, and was witnessed by a person now living in the parish.

Sometimes the bride-cake was tried for by persons on foot, and then it was called "throwing the quintal," which was performed with heavy bars of iron, thus affording a trial of muscular strength as well as of gallantry. This custom has been long discontinued, as well as the other.

The only custom now remaining at weddings that tends to recall a classical image to the mind is that of sending to a disappointed lover a garland of willow variously ornamented, accompanied sometimes with a pair of gloves, a white handkerchief, and a smelling-bottle.

Brand's "Antiquities," i., p. 124; ii., p. 155.
Macaulay's "Claybrook," pp. 130, 131.

WEDDING
CUSTOMS.

[Reprinted, without acknowledgment or reference,
by "W. Sydney," in "Leicestershire N. and
Q.," iii., p. 42.
See Nichols, IV., 131.   Ed.]

Cushion-Dance.—Brand ("Popular Antiquities," ii., p. 162) quotes
an account of this dance from Playford's "Dancing-Master,"
which correctly describes it, the only exception being that real
names are used instead of "John" and "Joan Sanderson."

Evans, p. 134.

Glenfield.—An inhabitant of Glenfield (Mr. J. S. Ellis) remembers the custom of throwing chaff before the door of a wife-
beater.   Within the last forty years he has seen the garden of a
house almost filled with chaff — the house now occupied by
T. F. Johnson, Esq., Jr.

[For a similar custom in Gloucestershire, cf. "Notes and
Queries," First Series, i., pp. 245, 294, and County Folk-Lore
Printed Extracts, No. I., Folk-Lore Society, p. 16.   Ed.]

See also under "Local Customs" [Marcheta and
Leyrwit] [Borough English] and "Superstitions
Generally."

FUNERAL
CUSTOMS.

The body of Lord Lanesborough is buried half of it within and
half outside the churchyard at Swithland.

It is the custom to lock the front door and open the window
wide after a death in the house.

From Mr. J. D. Paul.

Salt placed on Dead Bodies.—It was a custom in Leicester and
its shire, yet continued, to place a dish or plate of salt on a corpse
to prevent its swelling and purging, as the term is.

"Gentleman's Magazine Library," "Superstitious
Beliefs and Customs," p. 198.

Mr. Bickerstaff described an object found in St. Mary's churchyard at Leicester, which he imagined to be a plate once charged

with salt. Another correspondent suggested that it may have been
a *patten* entombed in the coffin of some priest or incumbent of that
church.   *Ib.*, p. 198.

Chiming Bells at Funerals.—This custom . . . . lingered in
several parishes in Leicestershire until recently. At Frisby, it
was used until the year 1842; at Oadby, in the case of one family,*
until 1844; and at Sapcote, Mrs. Spencer, who died in the year
1847, expressed a wish that the bells should be chimed at her
funeral, and her wish was granted. At Saxelby, it is still the
rule for the bells to be chimed on the arrival of the funeral procession at the church gates, and to continue to be chimed until all
are within the church.

North, " Church Bells of Leicestershire," p. 109.

Mr. Crane, who died about 1738, was the first person in Melton
Mowbray for whom the bell tolled after death ; till then the custom
was for it to pass before, agreeably to the primitive institution.

Nichols, II., 250.

Funeral-Feasts.—Nichols relates a custom as followed at Bar-
well, at the funeral of Miss Anne Power, who died 29 September
1785. She was, he says, a wealthy maiden lady, and at her
funeral, "agreeably to the custom of the country on the interment
of spinsters, the corpse was welcomed to the church with a merry
peal; and an elegant entertainment was distributed to a numerous
circle of friends and neighbouring dependents."

Nichols's " Leicestershire," IV., 480, note.

Doles at Funerals.—"Ita tamen quod corpus meum ultra triduum
super terram minime præservetur; quoad pastum relinquo arbitrio
executorum meorum nolo tamen quod modum excedant."

" Stock's Market Harborough Records," p. 51 (quoting
will of Geoffrey le Scrope, who died in 1382).

---

* The oldest family supposed to live in this village, t   Ludlams, who claimed
the distinction of having the deceased members of the family " chimed to
church," and asserted that it had been the custom to do so from time immemorial.—*Ibid.*, p. 257.

2 5 ✳

Waltham-on-the-Wolds.—There used to be a number of *funeral garlands* hanging up about the church, in commemoration of the deaths of unmarried women.

> "Transactions of the Leicestershire Architectural and Archaeological Society," p. 422.

Exhibited at Kegworth, August 26, 1868, a loaf of bread 400 years old. This loaf was sent by Mrs. Soar, of Elvaston, to one of whose ancestors it was given as a *funeral dole* on the death of one of the Harrington family.

> "Transactions of the Leicestershire Architectural and Archaeological Society," p. 348.

Godeby.—In this parish, when any person dies, the baker goes about with bread, and gives to every house as many penny-loaves as there are persons in the family, also a piece of plum cake.

> Nichols, II., 196.
> [For *Doles at Stathern. See* Nichols, II., 357. Ed.]

Funeral Cakes.—In 1664-5 Mr. Palmer, the town clerk of Leicester, died; and at his funeral the corporation expended £1 10s. for cakes.—Chamberlain's Accounts for that year.

> "Transactions of the Leicestershire Architectural and Archaeological Societies," vol. i., p. 119.

Nichols, in his "History of Lancashire" (misprint for *Leicestershire*), ii., part i., p. 382, speaking of Waltham in Framland Hundred says: "In this church, under every arch, a garland is suspended: one of which is customarily placed there whenever any young unmarried woman dies."

> Quoted in Brand's "Popular Antiquities" (Bohn), ii., p. 302.

At Melton Mowbray all of the same street are invited to a funeral, because, according to the Saxon institution, they were all of the same bonfire.

> Nichols, IV., 131.

See also under "Superstitions Generally."

(c) GAMES.

Making Cheeses, is an amusement for children, practised by girls. The process consists in spinning round rapidly and then crouching down so as to distend the petticoats somewhat in the shape of a cheese. The performers occasionally sing a song, of which the refrain is, "Turn, cheeses, turn!" but I do not remember to have heard the example cited by Mr. Halliwell-Phillips.

Percy Society, vol. iv., p. 122.
Evans, p. 119.

Cob-nut.—Strings are passed through nuts, by which to use them in playing. Each player, in turn, holds his cob-nut up by the string to be "cobbed" at by the other, and the player who first breaks his adversary's nut is the winner of the game.

Evans, p. 126.
[*See* Mrs. Gomme, "British Games," I., 71-72. Ed.]

Fighting Cocks.—A cock is a snail-shell used in the game of fighting-cocks, which is played by pressing the points or noses of two snail-shells together till one of them breaks.

Evans, p. 126.
[*See* "Cogger." Mrs. Gomme, "British Games," 1., 77. Ed.]

Duck.— A boys' game, played with rounded stones or boulders.

Evans, p. 142.

Wiggle-waggle.—A party sit round a table under the presidency of a "Buck." Each person has his fingers clenched, and the thumb extended. "Buck" from time to time calls out as suits his fancy : "Buck says, thumbs up!" or, "Buck says, thumbs down!" or, "Wiggle-waggle." If he says, "thumbs up!" he places both hands on the table with the thumbs sticking straight

GAMES. up. If "thumbs down!" he rests his thumbs on the table with his hands up. If "wiggle-waggle!" he places his hands as in "thumbs up," but wags his thumbs nimbly. Everybody at the table has to follow the word of command on the instant, and any who fail to do so are liable to a forfeit.

Evans, p. 290.

Old Games.—In the "ordinance" or bye-laws made by the Corporation of Leicester in the year 1467, it was forbidden that anyone should play for silver at any of the following games, under pain of imprisonment: that is to say, at dice, "carding," hazarding, tennis, bowles, "pykkyng" with arrows, quoiting with horse-shoes, penny-prick, football, or chequer-in-the-mire. And this regulation was confirmed at a Common Hall in the 3rd Henry VII., when all persons were forbidden to play for money at dyce, cards, bowles, half-bowle, hasardynge, tennys, pryckyng with arrows, coytyng with stones, or coytyng with horse-shoese, penny-pryk, foteball, classhe-coyles, checker-in-the-mire, or shove-grote.

Kelly's "Notices," p. 181.

Cushion Dance.—See "Wedding Customs."
Shuttlecock and Battledore.—See "Shrovetide."
Whipping Toms, Shindy, Football, see "Local Customs" [Whipping Toms].
Threaa-the-Needle.—See "Whipping Toms."
Drawing Dun.—See "Proverbs."

[*For Bingo* (with Leicestershire tune), *Cat-gallows, Drop-hand-kerchief* (with Leicestershire song), *Hide and Wink*, and *Jolly Miller* (with Leicestershire song).

See Mrs. Gomme, "British Games," i., pp. 29, 33, 63, 110, 213, 290, 291. Ed.]

(d) LOCAL CUSTOMS.

The Swainmote.—The Swainmote (as Nichols prefers spelling the word, from its supposed derivation—a meeting of the swains) was assembled three times a year, and Spelman described it to be "Curia forestæ de rebus et delictis in forestâ accidentibus." The owners of the lordships of Whitwick, Groby, and Shepeshead only held these courts; but whether the other lords of the forest were subordinate to these, or held other courts, taking cognizance of similar matters, does not appear. Like all courts of high antiquity, the Swainmote was held in the open air—that of Whitwick near Sharpley Rocks, where the place may still be traced; that of Groby at Copt Oak; and that of Shepeshead on Ives Head.

SWAIN-
MOTE.

> "History and Antiquities of Charnwood Forest,"
> T. R. Potter, 1842, p. 3.

Swains' Hill.—Swains' Hill—a name which suggests the probability of the spot having been a Swainmote Court—lies at the foot of Ives Head; and at a little distance from the latter stands the Hangman's Stone, which furnishes the subject of a legend.

> *Ib.*, p. 177.

Swainmote Rock.—In this parish (Whitwick), and about two miles north-east of the village, is the Swainmote Rock, on which, in early times, the courts of the forest were held.

> *Ib.*, p. 156.

> See under "Hills," "Sacred Stones," "Oaks,"
> "Gartree Bush," "Stanywells."

The Foresters.—The foresters were sworn officers, and their duty was to watch over vert and venison, and to make presentments of all trespasses.

THE
FOREST.

THE
FOREST.

A forester was also taken for the wood ward: and every forester, when called at a justice-seat, had to kneel and present his horn, while the wood ward knelt and presented his axe.

Ib., p. 3.

Maker's Manor.—The small commoners and cottagers of the various townships around enjoyed the privileges which the free forest afforded. They had their fern-harvests, at which the fern was gathered and burnt to make ash-bells; they had their little pickings of gorse, brushwood, firewood, turf, and peat; they had the minor "waifs and strays" of the warren; more than all, they had "fleet foot on the Correi." Some had a few stunted cows and forest sheep—a horse, it may be, or a few asses, which carried coals or besoms to the surrounding towns. Regarding the forest as their inalienable right, they greatly resented the encroachments that seemed to be extending wider and wider, from the increased vigilance with which the warreners found it necessary to guard the land in the neighbourhood of the warrens. A spirit of dissatisfaction at these inroads into what they called their "Maker's manor" (I have the expression from a very old forester) first begun to develop itself among the cottagers of Shepeshead and Whitwick.

"History and Antiquities of Charnwood Forest,"
T. R. Potter, 1842, p. 23.

FREBORD.

In some, if not in all the manors in this vicinity in which this right exists, the quantity of ground claimed as *frebord* is thirty feet in width from the set of the hedges.

Leicestriensis in "Notes and Queries," vol. v. (1852),
p. 595.

HAY
STREWING.

Strewing Churches with Hay.—At Glenfield, according to Edwards ("Old English Customs and Charities"), the parish clerk, in accordance with an old custom, strews the church with new hay on the first Sunday after the 5th of July in each year.[*] This is probably

---

[*] Quoted in Dyer's "British Popular Customs" (Bohn), p. 338, from Edwards' "Old English Customs and Charities," p. 219. Ed.

a survival of the ancient English practice of strewing the floors of not only churches, but dwelling-houses also, with hay, straw, or rushes. When the first Norman monarch occupied the throne of this realm, he gave to one of his subjects a grant of land in return for supplying him with "straw for his bedchamber," and in summer straw and rushes twice a year, besides other tributary payments. Hentzner, in his "Itinerary," says of Queen Elizabeth's presence chamber: "The floor, after the English fashion, was strewed with hay. . . . . The same curious custom is also observed at the church in the adjoining village of Braunston, which is ecclesiastically connected with Glenfield."—S.

"Leicestershire Notes and Queries," vol. i., p. 119.

On July 6th this year (1890), the Sunday after St. Peter's Day, being the feast, the church at Braunston was as usual strewn with hay, as has been the wont from time immemorial. The origin of this, as of many other singular customs, is lost in the mists of antiquity. On the Thursday before the wake, or feast, the "Holme" meadow (one of eight situated near St. Mary's Mills, seven of which are on the east side of the River Soar) is mown, and the parish clerk of Braunston fetches therefrom on the Saturday a small load of hay, which he must spread with his hands (without using a fork) on the floor of the church. The portion of the meadow from which the hay is taken is marked out with a stake, and called "the clerk's acre," the whole of the crop thereon being claimed by that functionary, but the tenant usually has it by paying him the sum of thirty shillings. Another acre is claimed by the rector of Aylestone, who receives from the tenant the sum of two guineas as a modus, instead of the produce thereof.

Some years ago, while the church was undergoing extensive repairs and roofless, the then rector of Aylestone deputed some one to pay a visit at the time appointed, thir   the pai   clerk would omit the annual custom, but *he* was not to be caught napping. In all probability, in default of continuance of the same, there would be tithe or some other payment claimed on the whole.

HAY
STREWING.

From the situation of these fields, beyond the River Soar, a natural boundary, apparently an outline of the parish, it is possible that at some distant date they may have belonged to or had some connection with the adjoining parish of Aylestone.

In the early part of the century it was the custom to take the hay required from the "clerk's acre," to Braunston "the way the crow flies," that is, across the River Soar, through cornfields, hedges, and ditches, and this was annually made the occasion for a rough and boisterous holiday.

Singular to relate, although Throsby mentions briefly this custom in his excursions, Nichols, in his voluminous "County History," makes no mention thereof.

R. B

[The Editors are obliged for these particulars from one who was formerly a tenant for many years.]

"Leicestershire Notes and Queries," vol. i., p. 265.

[*See* "Charity Reports," xxxii., pt. x., p. 158 ; and Burton's "Rush-bearing," 1891, p. 22.   Ed.]

Hay Strewing at Ashby Folville.—The floor of this church used formerly to be strewn with hay or rushes from the first Sunday in August until Christmas, which custom continued until the early part of the present century, when the piece of land (about one rood) whence the hay was procured was let to the tenant who occupied the rest of the field at a small rent. It was a triangular piece of land marked out by three large stones, in a field called "The Bartlemews," situate between Ashby Pastures and Thorpe Thrussels. It is traditionally reported that two ladies, being benighted, and having lost their way, heard the bells of the place ring, and thus found their way to the village ; and, on the spot where they heard the bells, they dropped a handkerchief, where the next day it was found. The produce of the land was in consequence appropriated yearly for the church in commemoration of their escape from danger. The oldest record I have seen of it (about 1745) states that the parishioners of Ashby Folville have the right of the grass growing on this land to strew their church with in winter. The land has recently been sold to the owner of the other part of the field; and part of the money expended in repairing the church windows, Barsby. T. Randall. **HAY STREWING.**

"Leicestershire Notes and Queries," vol. ii., p. 254.

Wymondham.—The Wake is now kept the Sunday following the feast of S. Peter, when the church is always strewed with rushes, and the parish clerk is paid 1s. 6d. out of a farm, for what is called "Church-grass."

Nichols, II., 406.

Medbourne.—An annual custom prevailed at Medbourn, discontinued but about eight or ten years, of strewing new hay along the aisles of the church on the last Sunday in June or first in July.

Nichols, III., 539.

The " Whipping Toms."—Another ancient custom, now abolished, was the sport known as *Whipping Toms*, which was held in that part of the precincts of Leicester Castle called the *Newarke*, originally the *New Work*, an area of considerable extent. **WHIPPING TOMS.**

I have myself on several occasions, when a boy, witnessed this singular spectacle from the garden of one of the houses in the Newarke. The sports usually began about ten or eleven o'clock in the morning of Shrove Tuesday, the principal game being that of "Shinney" or "Hockey." * All other proceedings were, however, superseded by the Whipping Toms, who commenced operations at one o'clock. After that hour any persons passing through the Newarke were liable to be whipped, unless they paid a fee to any or all of the Whipping Toms by whom they might be met or pursued, who, however, were not by custom allowed to whip above the knee, and any one kneeling down was safe from attack so long as he remained in that posture.

* Described by Mr. Halliwell, in his " Archaic Dictionary," under the name of " Bandy."

Many of the lower class, and occasionally some "fast" young fellows of the middle class (who came "to see the fun"), would take what was called "two pennyworth of whipping," or, in other words, would take part in a kind of *fencing match*—the Whipping Tom endeavouring to whip their legs with his long cart-whip, and the others endeavouring to ward off the blows with their long sticks with all the skill of which they were master. Occasionally a well-directed blow would take effect, the stroke often cutting through the stocking * of the unskilful or incautious recipient. On these occasions a ring would be formed round the pair of antagonists, and whilst the attention of the spectators was engrossed by the exciting contest going on before their eyes, they would be suddenly startled by the warning sound of the bells, and find themselves attacked in the rear by other Whipping Toms, when they would scamper in all directions; sometimes, however, by surrounding the bellman, they would succeed in silencing "that awful bell," and thus, for a time, render the Whipping Tom powerless, until one of his companions, with his attendant bell, should rush to the rescue.

The "bounds," beyond which everyone was safe from attack, were the *Magazine* Gateway, the *Turret* Gateway, the lane leading to *Rupert's* Tower (part of the old town wall), and the passage between Trinity Hospital and St. Mary's Vicarage, leading to the pike-yard, which it seems was at one time "dignified by the name of Little London." †

It was formerly the custom on this day for the lads and lasses to meet in the spacious gallery of the women's ward in Trinity Hospital, and to play at "Thread-the-Needle," and other similar games. This, however, from its annoying the aged inmates, was discontinued a few years before the *sport* of Whipping Toms was finally abolished. All attempts to put a stop to the practice of this ancient custom (which certainly was one "more honoured in

---

* See Mr. W. Gardiner's "Music and Friends," vol. i., p. 366.

† As stated in a communication to Hone's "Year Book" (p. 539) on this subject.

the breach than the observance ") had proved futile; until, at length, the aid of an Act of Parliament was called in to abolish it, a clause with that object being embodied in the "Leicester Improvement Act," which received the Royal Assent on the 18th June, 1846. As this clause (the 41st) clearly indicates the strong hold which this annual sport retained upon many of the people, even at that recent period, it is here given :—

"Whereas a certain custom or practice called 'Whipping Toms' has for many years existed in a public place called the Newarke, in the said borough, on Shrove Tuesday, which has caused large numbers of people to assemble there, who, by the sport there carried on, occasion great noise and inconvenience, not only to persons residing in the Newarke, but to the inhabitants of the said borough generally, by preventing persons not engaged in the said sports from passing along the said place without subjecting themselves to the payment of money, which is demanded of them to escape being whipped : Be it therefore enacted, That from and after the passing of this Act the said custom or practice called Whipping Toms shall be and the same is hereby declared to be unlawful; and in case any person or persons shall, on Shrove Tuesday in any year after the passing of this Act, play at Whipping Toms, shindy, football, or any other game on any part of the said place called the Newarke, or stand, or be in the said place with any whip, stick, or other instrument for the purpose of playing thereat, he or they shall forfeit or pay for every such offence any sum not exceeding the sum of five pounds, to be recovered in like manner as other penalties created by this Act; and it shall be lawful for any police constable or peace officer of the said borough without any warrant whatsoever to seize and apprehend any person offending as aforesaid, and forthwith to convey him before any justice of the peace, in order to his conviction for the said offence."

On the Shrove Tuesday following the passing of this Act, although due notice had been given to the public of the consequences, great numbers of the "roughs" among the working-

classes, together with the old Whipping Toms, assembled in the
Newarke, with the determination to have their sport as usual,
and it was only after a serious collision between the police and the
people, during which many heavy blows were given and returned,
that the authorities at length succeeded in clearing the Newarke,
several of the ringleaders in the affair being taken into
custody.

Thus, by force of law, in the middle of the nineteenth century,
was brought to an end the unique sport of Whipping Toms ; a
custom whose origin and meaning are lost in the mists of
antiquity, for on these points all is conjecture, nor do we find any
clear traces of a similar custom existing at any period in other
parts of the kingdom.

One local tradition is, that it was instituted to commemorate
the expulsion of the Danes from Leicester, on Hoke Day
A.D. 1002, when nearly all the Danes in England were
massacred. * Another, and, we think, a much more plausible
theory, is, that it owes its origin to John of Gaunt, and that it was
a tenure by which certain privileges granted by him to the
inhabitants of the locality were maintained,† the Newarke—in
which stood the collegiate church (the burial place of the House of
Lancaster), the houses of the canons, and the hospital founded by
Earl Henry in 1330—as well as " the Castle View," on the northward side of the castle—having been, until very recently, extra-
parochial. We have already alluded to the still more barbarous
custom of " Bull-running " at Tutbury, which, it seems probable,
was instituted by John of Gaunt; and, from the very curious
ceremonies which he prescribed to be observed as the tenure by
which the land he conferred upon certain Ratby men was to be
held, in commemoration of a romantic incident which is related at
length by Throsby,‡ and which ceremonies are still, in part, kept
up, we may conclude that this celebrated man had a considerable

---

* Thompson's " History of Leicester," p. 18 (note).
† Gardiner's " Music and Friends," vol. i., p. 366.
‡ " Leicestershire Views," vol. ii., pp. 83-86.

spice of eccentricity in his disposition, and that his great WHIPPING
popularity in the neighbourhood was due, in some degree, to the TOMS.
freedom with which he occasionally mingled in the sports of the
people.

The only use of the term " Whipping Tom " we have met with
elsewhere than in Leicester, is in a quotation from Aubrey, in
Thoms' " Anecdotes and Traditions," * where mention is made of
"A Whipping Tom in Kent, who disciplined the wandering maids
and women till they were afraid to walk abroad." Upon this
passage Mr. Thoms observes :—" ' Whipping Tom's Rod for a
Proud Lady ' is the title of a satirical tract, published about the
year 1744. Whipping Tom himself," adds the learned editor,
" would appear to bear some resemblance to Mumbo Jumbo, ' who
disciplined the wandering maids and women' of Africa."

The great antiquity, the unknown origin, and the unique
character of this curious local sport, coupled with its being now
entirely obsolete, have led to its being dilated upon at far greater
length than its rude nature would otherwise have merited.

Kelly's " Notices of Leicester," pp. 174-180.

Strutt, in his " Sports and Pastimes " . . . omits giving a
description of an ancient custom at Leicester, called the Whipping
Toms. Within the precincts of the castle there is a large open
space called the Newarke, where crowds of the lower orders
resort on Shrove Tuesday for a holiday. In my father's time
the sports were cock-throwing, single-stick, wrestling, &c.; and
probably the practice we are about to speak of arose from a
difficulty in clearing the square of the people in order to close the
gates. On the ringing of the bell, crowds, chiefly young persons,
begin to assemble, armed with long sticks, used only as weapons
of defence. About three o'clock the Whipping Toms arrive; three
stout fellows, furnished with cart-whips, and a man with a bell
runs before them to give notice of their approach. The bell
sounding, the floggers begin to strike in every direction, to drive
the rabble out at the gates; but they are opposed and set at

* Printed for the Camden Society, p. 101.

2 6

WHIPPING TOMS. defiance by hundreds of men and boys, who defend their legs with sticks. The mob so tease and provoke the flagellators that they lay about them unmercifully, often cutting through the stockings of the assailants at a stroke. This amusement, if so it can be called, is continued for several hours, the combatants being driven from one end of the garrison to the other, surrounded by crowds of idle women and spectators. Attempts have been made to get rid of this rude custom, but without effect, as some tenure is maintained by it.

> Chambers' " Book of Days," vol. i., p. 365-6.
>
> [*See also* Throsby "History of Leicester," 1791, p. 356. Dyer's " British Popular Customs " (Bohn), p. 79. " Leaflets from my Life," by Mary Kirby (an eye-witness) (London: Simpkin, Marshall, & Co. 1887), pp. 11-12. "Leicestershire N. and Q." vol. iii., p. 29. Hone's Year Book, 1838, pp. 536-7.
>
> Aubrey's " Remaines of Gentilisme" (Folk-Lore Society, 1880), p. 59, as to Whipping Toms in Kent, and Note on p. 228.
>
> Mrs. Gomme's " Traditional Games," vol. i., pp. 217-218. Ed.]

Whipping Toms.—The account is so very complete that I think it is a pity not to add one more particular, viz.: that the spot on which the mayor stood to address the mob is still marked in the pavement of the street.

Perhaps the stones will not always be there; would it not be well to record that they were existing in 1893?

From Miss H. Ellis.

PUBLIC PENANCE. Between six and seven years ago, a man and a woman in this parish were presented by the churchwardens in the spiritual court for fornication; and they both did public penance by standing in the middle aisle, during the time of divine service, invested with white sheets.

Macaulay's " Claybrook," p. 132.

A stranger looking on at workmen engaged in their work, **FOOTING.**
will generally be asked to "pay his footing," or "stand his foot-
ale." A workman is also often expected to pay his footing on
joining a gang.

Evans, p. 153.

[This happened at the last general election to a Parliamentary
candidate who went to address some quarrymen at Enderby, and
who was not allowed to depart without paying his footing. It
was afterwards brought up against him by the other side as
bribery and corruption. Ed.]

The first time a peer of the realm comes within the precinct **HORSE-**
of the manor of Oakham, he forfeits a shoe from his horse, **SHOES AT**
to be nailed on the castle gate; and, should he refuse it or **OAKHAM.**
a compensation in money, the bailiff is empowered to take it
by force. This custom originated at the first erection of the
castle in the reign of Henry II., as a token of the territorial
power of its lord, Walthien de Ferrers, whose ancestor, who
came over with William the Conqueror, bore for arms, *Argent, six
horse shoes pierced sable*; designative of his office as Master of the
Horse to the Dukes of Normandy. These shoes, or rather the
shoes purchased with the compensation money, are now nailed
within the walls of the castle, and some are of a very elaborate
and historical character, each bearing the date and the name of
the donor.

W. C.

"Leicestershire Notes and Queries," vol. i. p. 63.
[*See also ib.* ii., 185, " The Hall of Oakham."]

As a supplement to W. C.'s note on this subject, the following
further particulars may be acceptable :—

"The walls are literally covered by memorials of princes and
peers who have paid tribute to the custom of the country. Over
the old oaken chair (occupied by the judge of assize when he
attends to receive a pair of white gloves, as a token that the

HORSE-
SHOES AT
OAKHAM.

country cannot produce a delinquent for judicial censure), is an immense shoe, constructed of solid brass, erected in 1814, and bearing the name of the Prince Regent. Near it are the tokens of Queen Elizabeth and the Princess of Wales, the latter placed on the wall in 1881. Her Majesty the Queen also left a souvenir of her visit to the county nineteen years ago, which occupies a place adjoining those of the Princess of Wales, and the Duke of York. Lord Coleridge, the Duke of Cambridge, Lord Lonsdale, Earl Dysart, the Marquis of Huntley, the Earl of Gainsborough, the Earl of Cardigan, the Duke of Norfolk, Bishop of Carlisle, Baron Raglan, and the romantic Earl of Exeter, have also paid the usual penalty for entering this peculiar county. In every instance but one the horseshoes are of fancy construction, the exception being afforded by that of Lord Willoughby, the shoe at present affixed being taken from the foot of a favourite horse, "Clinker," that earned for its owner considerable fame on the turf. The Iron Duke in his peaceful days was caught on the borders of the county, and the shoe with his name painted upon it betrays that he was unable to resist the advances of the impulsive Oakhamites. It will be difficult, from its very peculiarity, to discover in this land of castles a relic so astonishing."

"Leicestershire Notes and Queries, vol. i., pp. 106-107.

[*See* a Paper on "Horseshoe Customs at Oakham, Rutland," by Dr. J. Evans, P.S.A., read before the Society of Antiquaries of London on March 3rd, 1892, and published in "Leicestershire Notes and Queries," vol. iii., p. 15. Ed.]

CURFEW-
BELL.

Curfew-bell is rung at Barrow-on-Soar; Belgrave (in winter); Bottesford (excepting during Whitsun-week); Burbage (in winter); Burton-Overy; Claybrook (discontinued); Glen Magna (discontinued); Hinckley (winter); Kegworth (winter); St. Martin's, Leicester; St. Mary's, Leicester (discontinued); Lockington (winter); All Saints, Loughborough; Lutterworth; Market Harborough (discontinued); Melton Mowbray (from Michaelmas

to Lady Day); Rotherby (discontinued); Shepeshead (winter); CURFEW-
Shepey Magna (winter, excepting during the interval between the BELL.
death and burial of any parishioner); Sibstone (winter); Stoke
Golding (formerly); Waltham-on-the-Wolds; Whetstone (discontinued).

From North's " Church Bells of Leicestershire," pp.
134-309.

Curfew-bell is rung at Langham; Luffenham (South); and
Oakham.

From North's " Church Bells of Rutland," pp. 118-
166.

Gleaning-bell is rung at Ashwell; Bisbrooke (discontinued); GLEANING
Braunstone; Great Casterton; Clipsham; Cottesmore; Egleton; BELL.
Empingham; Greetham; Hambleton; Langham; Lyddington;
Manton (discontinued); Market Overton; Morcot; Oakham;
Seaton (discontinued); Tickencote (discontinued); Whissendine;
Whitwell.

From North's " Church Bells of Rutland," pp. 118-
166.

In several country parishes, as at Waltham-on-the-Wolds
and Wymondham, a gleaning-bell is rung during harvest, both
morning and evening, giving warning when gleaning may commence, and when it must close for the day.

North's " Church Bells of Leicestershire," p. 120.

I am glad to see an ancient custom revived in this village of HARVEST
electing from amongst themselves a Queen of the Gleaners. CUSTOM.
When elected, she is borne in a chair to the first field that is to
be gleaned; a crown, composed of wild flowers and a few ears of
corn is placed upon her head, and she tells her laws to her subjects. They are informed that when there are fields to be gleaned,
a horn or bell will summon them to the outskirts of the village,
and that she will then conduct them to the field. The Queen then

HARVEST
CUSTOM

stipulates for a sum to be paid to her attendants, who undertake to summon the gleaners.

She next impresses upon her people the necessity of obedience to her as their head, and of union among themselves. The infirmities of the aged are mentioned, and the cares of the cottage are not forgotten. The rustic sovereign then declares "her will and pleasure" to the effect that her people "shall not stray from the field" to which she "leads them"; and that any one who violates this law "shall forfeit her gathering, and her corn shall be bestrewed." Wishing for all a good harvest, and that they "may glean it in peace," the Queen is then borne from the field to the end of the village surrounded by her subjects, and conveyed home admidst mirth and song.

> [From a letter from a native of Rempston, Loughborough, to the Editor of the "Leicester Guardian," October 17th, 1859.]

MARCHETA
AND
LEYRWIT.

William de Moldestone held land in Keton, Rutland, of Hasculph de Whitewelle in villenage (5th Ed. III.) rendering (*inter alia*), "to the Lord five shillings for the *Marcheta*, if his (the tenant's) daughter should be married, and five shillings for *Leyrwit*, if she should commit fornication."

> Blore's "Rutland," p. 229.

Waltham.—All the women in villanage paid him (Alan de Nevile) *Merchet* and *Lotherwit*.

> Nichols, II., 380.

GUILDS.

Origin.—A meeting of the Guild was originally known in the (Leicester) rolls by the name "morwen speche," which is traceable to the ancient term "morgen spaec," employed to designate the "morning speeches," or heathen festivals, of primæval Germany, from which the subsequent meetings of Anglo-Saxon England may be supposed to have been derived. As every consultation was connected with a convivial feast amongst the early Germans, and a common building was constructed in which the rude banquets and deliberations of the less wealthy freemen

were held, the name of which (*domus conviviae*) implied thus GUILDS.
much, so their descendants in this country appear to have introduced the " morwen speche " and the Guild-hall with their other
customs.   In Leicester, the entries on the Guild, introducing the
matters recorded, sometimes commence in this style : " Haec est
le morwen speche de la Gild," thus intermingling Latin, German,
and French in the same sentence ; the writer being unable to
substitute for the words " morwen speche " and " Gild " any
French or Latin equivalents, and thereby unconsciously proving
their Teutonic origin.

Thompson's " English Municipal History," p. 49.

We learn from the rolls of the Guild Merchant of Leicester
that usually once a year the members met in their hall to
admit new members and to transact other business.   At their
head sat the alderman, or aldermen ; for sometimes one person is
mentioned, sometimes two are noticed.   The custom was to require
the initiate to take an oath of fealty to the Guild ; to find two
pledges or securities for the fulfilment of his obligations ; to pay
a fee on entrance ; a contribution for the bull ; a payment to the
" hause," and smaller ones not specified.   Having complied with
these requirements, the new member was called a brother of the
Guild, was entitled to enjoy all its advantages, was liable to discharge all its corresponding responsibilities, and was eligible to
fill its offices.

ib. p. 50.

The payment for the bull will be well understood when it is
remembered that many of the members of the Guild depastured
cows on the common near the town ; while the contribution to the
" hause " seems only to relate to the periodical subscription to
the Guild—the word " hause " and the word " Guild " being
synonymous.

ib. p. 52.

When the son of a member of the Guild was admitted, it

GUILDS.   was under favourable circumstances; he was said to have
"the seat of his father," and no payments were required.
Thus :—

> " Ralph, son of Jocelyn, has the seat of his father,
> Simon with the beard has the seat of his father."

In the case of the servants of members of the Guild, a similar
freedom from fees appears to have been occasionally allowed, as is
here exemplified :—

> "Geoffrey, the man of Osmond the Tailor, is quit of entrance fee."

The son of a priest was placed in a similar position—*Osmond
filius sacerdotis* being admitted without payment of fees.

Finally, concerning the members of the Guild, it may be
remembered that they constituted the "burgesses" of the town,
and none other.

Thompson's "English Municipal History," pp. 52, 53.

BOROUGH-   A usage, called the law of Borough English, had long
ENGLISH.   prevailed in Leicester, in accordance with which the youngest
son succeeded to the property of his father. It was alleged
that owing to a defect of heirs and their weakness, the town
was falling into ruin and dishonour, and therefore a change in
the established custom was necessary. The burgesses accordingly supplicated the Earl to grant them a charter, under the
authority of which their eldest-born sons might succeed to the
paternal inheritance and habitation—to what has been already
legally designated "the burgage." The Earl listened to the
prayer, and granted the charter requested, which was dated at
Westminster, in the month of October, 1255.

Thompson's "English Municipal History," p. 62.

HAM-   The succeeding passages in the document of which these
SOCKENS.   paragraphs form an abridgment (Agreement of 1281 A.D.),

relate to the compulsory expulsion from the town of Leicester HAM-
of persons who were "bold to make bates, batteries, and ham- SOCKENS.
sockens" (which last word means the assaulting of men in their
own houses—a very serious offence in the estimation of our
ancestors).

Thompson's "English Municipal History," p. 67.

[See "House-Peace": read before the Incorporated
Law Society at their Annual Meeting, 1893,
and published in their Report.—Ed.]

At the end of this street (High Cross Street) the name of High HIGH
Cross is still given to a plain Doric pillar, which, till the year CROSS
1773 (when it was in so ruinous a state as to be dangerous and an FAIR.
annoyance to the passage in the street it stood in), formed one of
the supporters of a light temple-looking building of the same
name . . . . which served as a shelter to the country people who
here hold a small market on Wednesdays and Fridays for the sale
of butter, eggs, &c.* Here the members of Parliament are pro-
claimed. Here also may be seen, on Michaelmas Day, the
grotesque ceremony of the poor men of Trinity Hospital, arrayed
like antient knights, having rusty helmets on their heads, and
breast-plates fastened on thin black tabards, proclaiming the
fair.

Nichols' Leicestershire, vol. I., p. 532.

The story that the Mayor (of Leicester) is chosen by a sow. MAYOR OF
The candidates sit each with his hat full of beans in his lap, and LEICESTER
he is the Mayor from whose hat the sow eats first. CHOSEN BY
A SOW.

Southey's "Commonplace Book," 4th Series 1851,
p. 341, quoting "St. James's Magazine," 1762,
vol. ii., p. 13.

See "Nicknames" [Beanbelly Leicestershire.]

---

* Removed a few years ago. Ed.

MOP FAIR
AT SAP-
COTE.

It is a custom in this parish once every year for certain of the young people to go out in the night through the whole village, after the inhabitants are gone to bed, and take all the mops, besoms, and brushes they can find carelessly left out of doors, and throw them into the horse-pit in the middle of the town. The next morning is called *Mop-fair*, and it is a ludicrous sight to see the old women and servant-maids from all parts of the town examining the pit for their scrubbing utensils, of which the best are generally taken first.

Nichols, IV., 898.

HIGH
CROSS.

The youth of the adjoining counties of Leicester and Warwick used formerly to meet at this place (at the intersection of Fosse Road and Watling Street on the borders of Warwickshire, Ed.) for the purpose of performing the athletic exercises of wrestling, singlestick playing, &c.; but these games began to be discontinued about the year 1750, and the remembrance of them now is almost obliterated.

Nichols, IV., 915.

See also under Part I. (a) (b) ; Part II. (a) (b) (c).

Part III.

TRADITIONAL NARRATIVES.

(a) DROLLS.

A small boy was one day eating plum cake, when he said to his mother— HUMBLE-CUM-BUZZ.

"Oi sa', moother, ha' plooms got legs?"

"Nooa, ma lad!"

"Then, moother, ah'v swallered a 'oomble-coom-booz!"

Evans, p. 175.

"The paason, ah suppose a wanted to mek a Epril fule on me; a says, 'John,' a says, 'ha' ye heerd what's 'appened Hinckley wee?' Soo ah says, 'Noo, ah een't heerd nothink,' ah says. 'Whoy,' a says, 'they wur a-diggin' a well ober by theer,' a says, 'an' the bottom fell out!' 'Hoo,' ah says, 'did it? An' wheer did it goo tow?' Soo a says, 'Ah dunna knoo, John,' a says. Soo ah says, 'Well,' ah says, 'if yo dunna knoo, yo may goo luke.'" THE BOTTOM-LESS WELL.

Evans, p. 93.

Gotham is a parish now containing seven or eight hundred inhabitants, and though in the county of Nottingham, is close on the borders of Leicestershire. THE WISE MEN OF GOTHAM.

"Leicestershire N. and Q.," ii. 177.

THE WISE MEN OF GOTHAM.

The story of *the Hare that took the Rent* has some local colour.

[See Clouston's " Book of Noodles," p. 27. Ed.]

THE MONK OF LEICESTER.

".A merry jest of Dane Hew, monk of Leicester, and how he was foure times slain and once hanged."

[*See* W. C. Hazlitt's " National Tales and Legends," p. 480.

Old English metrical version preserved in the Bodleian. (London: John Allder, M.D., no date, probably about 1450, Clouston. Nichols has the date 1596).

Clouston's " Popular Tales and Fictions," vol. ii., p. 353.

Nichols' " History of Leicestershire," vol. I., part 2, p. 287.

The story is the wide-spread tale of the Hunchback in the " Arabian Nights." " The localization of the story was a common expedient when old wares were served up again," Hazlitt. Clouston thinks the tale must have been directly derived from Jean le Chapelain's *fabliau* of " Le Sacristan de Cluni.' Ed.]

(*b*) PLACE LEGENDS AND TRADITIONS.

THE GIANT BEL.

The Giant Bel.—" In Domesday Book Belgrave appears as Merdegrave, and the transformation which converted it into Belgrave, was, it is fair to infer, the work of a Norman owner. This change of name subsequent to the Conquest unfortunately precludes us from assigning any very high antiquity to the local legend with regard to a certain giant Bel, whose name, as might have been expected, has proved a snare to more than one topographical antiquary. Bel, we learn, vowed that he would

reach Leicester from Mountsorrel in three leaps. He accordingly **THE GIANT**
mounted his sorrel steed at Mountsorrel. One leap carried him **BEL.**
as far as Wanlip in safety, but on essaying a second he burst all
—his harness, his horse, and himself—at Burstall. In spite of this
misadventure Bel drove his spurs into his dying charger, and
attempted the third leap. But the effort was too great. Steed
and rider dropped dead together a mile and a half short of
Leicester, and were buried together in one grave at Belgrave.
This legend, the historic accuracy of which is of course placed
beyond doubt by the still existing names of the various stages in
the giant's inauspicious journey, is certainly more than two
centuries old, and, whatever may be its value in other respects,
proves that during that period, at least, the Leicestershire
pronunciation of 'one' and 'leap' has remained unchanged."

Evans, p. 42-3.

See also under "Place Rhymes."

King Lear.—"After this unhappy fate of Bladud, Leir, his son, **LEAR.**
was advanced to the throne, and nobly governed his country sixty
years. He built upon the river Sore a city, called in the British
tongue, Kaerleir, in the Saxon, Leircestre. He was without male
issue, but had three daughters, whose names were Gonorilla, Regan,
and Cordeilla, of whom he was dotingly fond, but especially of his
youngest Cordeilla." . . . .

(Here follows the story of King Lear and his three daughters,
quoted from Geoffrey in "Holinshed's Chronicles," and there read
by Shakespeare. The story concludes thus):—

"Cordeille, obtaining the government of the kingdom, buried her
father in a certain vault, which she ordered to be made for him
under the river Sore, in Leicester, and which had been built
originally under the ground to the honour of the god Janus. And
here all the workmen of the city, upon the anniversary solemnity
of that festival, used to begin their yearly labours."

Geoffrey of Monmouth's "British History," Book II.
cp. xi.-xiv.
Bohn's Antiquarian Library, "Six Old English
Chronicles," 1848, pp. 114-119.

K

King Lear.—The tale of King Lear and his three Daughters as given by Holinshed in "An Historical Description of the Island of Bretayne," 1509, on the authority of Matthew of Westminster and Geoffrey of Monmouth, is connected with Leicester.

"Hee made the towne of Caerleir nowe called Leicester, which standeth upon ye River of Sore."

"His body was buried at Leicester in a vault under ye channel of the River of Sore beneath the towne."

Matthew of Westminster tells the story of Lear without mentioning Leicester except at the end of the narrative, where he writes :—

"Cordelia, the daughter of the king, succeeded to the helm of the kingdom, and buried her father in a subterraneous cave, which she had commanded to be made in Leicester beneath the river Sera."

> Matthew of Westminster's Chronicle "Flowers of
> History" (Bohn, 1853), I. 49.
> (*See* Nichols, I., pp. 2, 3.)

New Park.—There is in the Park a cave digged out of the rock, where it is said King Leyer did hide himself from his enemies.

> Nichols, IV., 784.

See also under "Superstitions."

(*c*) FOLK-DRAMA.

MUMMER'S PLAY.

The Mummer's Play, as performed in some of the villages near Lutterworth, at Christmas, 1863.

DRAMATIS PERSONÆ.

1. CAPTAIN SLASHER, *in military costume, with sword and pistol.*
2. KING OF ENGLAND, *in robes, wearing the crown.*

3. Prince George, *King's son, in robes, and sword by his side.*
4. Turkish Champion, *in military attire, with sword and pistol.*
5. A Noble Doctor.
6. Beelzebub.
7. A Clown.

Enter Captain Slasher.

I beg your pardon for being so bold,
I enter your house, the weather's so cold,
Room, a room! brave gallants! give us room to sport;
For in this house we do resort,—
Resort, resort, for many a day;
Step in, the King of England,
And boldly clear the way.

Enter King of England.

I am the King of England, that boldly does appear;
I come to seek my only son—my only son is here.

Enter Prince George.

I am Prince George, a worthy knight;
I'll spend my blood for England's right.
England's right I will maintain;
I'll fight for old England once again.

Enter Turkish Knight.

I am the Turkish Champion,
From Turkey's land I come;
I come to fight the King of England
And all his noble men.

Captain Slasher.

In comes Captain Slasher,
Captain Slasher is my name,
With sword and pistol by my side
I hope to win the game.

KING OF ENGLAND.

I am the King of England,
As you may plainly see,
These are my soldiers standing by me;
They stand by me your life to end
On them doth my life depend.

PRINCE GEORGE.

I am Prince George, the champion bold,
And with my sword I won three crowns of gold
I slew the fiery dragon and brought him to the slaughter,
And won the King of Egypt's only daughter.

TURKISH CHAMPION

As I was going by St. Francis's School,
I heard a lady cry "A fool, a fool!"
"A fool," was every word,
"That man's a fool
Who wears a wooden sword."

PRINCE GEORGE.

A wooden sword, you dirty dog!
My sword is made of the best of metal free.
If you would like to taste of it,
I'll give it unto thee.
Stand off, stand off, you dirty dog!
Or by my sword you'll die.
I'll cut you down the middle
And make your blood to fly.

[*They fight; Prince George falls, mortally wounded.*

Enter KING OF ENGLAND.

Oh, horrible! terrible! what hast thou done?
Thou hast ruin'd me, ruin'd me,
By killing of my only son.

Oh! Is there ever a noble doctor to be found,
To cure this English champion
Of his deep and deadly wound.

Enter NOBLE DOCTOR.

Oh, yes; there is a noble doctor to be found,
To cure this English champion
Of his deep and deadly wound.

KING OF ENGLAND.

And pray what is your practice?

NOBLE DOCTOR.

I boast not of my practice, neither do I study
In the practice of physic.

KING OF ENGLAND.

What can you cure?

NOBLE DOCTOR.

All sorts of diseases.
Whatever you pleases:
I can cure the itch, the pitch,
The phthisic, the palsy, and the gout;
And if the devil's in the man,
I can fetch him out.
My wisdom lies in my wig,
I torture not my patients with excations,
Such as pills, boluses, solutions, and embrocations,
But by the word of command
I can make this mighty prince to stand.

KING.

What is your fee?

DOCTOR.

Ten pounds is true.

KING.

Proceed, noble Doctor:
You shall have your due.

DOCTOR.

Arise, arise! most noble prince, arise,
And no more dormant lay;
And with thy sword
Make all thy foes obey.

[The Prince arises.

PRINCE GEORGE.

My head is made of iron,
My body is made of steel,
My legs are made of crooked bones
To force you all to yield

Enter BEELZEBUB.

In comes I, old Beelzebub,
Over my shoulder I carry my club,
And in my hand a frying-pan,
Pleased to get all the money I can.

Enter CLOWN.

In comes I, who's never been yet,
With my great head and little wit:
My head is great, my wit is small,
I'll do my best to please you all.

SONG (*all join*).

And now we are done and must be gone
No longer will we stay here;

But if you please, before we go,
We'll taste your Christmas beer. [*]

[*Exeunt omnes.*

Several versions of the play of St. George, as represented at
Chiswick and the neighbourhood, in Worcestershire, and in
Hampshire, will be found in "Notes and Queries," 2nd Series,
vols. x., xi., and xii. respectively; that acted in the West of
England is printed in Sandy's "Christmas Tide," and that used
at Whitehaven in Hone's "Year Book," vol. ii., 1646. All these,
while agreeing in substance, vary in some respects from each
other, both as regards the characters and words, whilst the
Leicestershire version has an affinity to the whole of them,
showing one common origin.

Kelly's "Notices of Leicester," pp. 53-57.

Robin Hood's Play at Melton.—The following transcripts, from
the original MSS. Accounts of the Churchwardens of Melton
Mowbray (in the possession of William Latham, Esq.) are probably
not surpassed by those of any town, as curious memorials of that
popular amusement of the age to which they belong, whilst
locally they possess the additional interest of appertaining to
this county.

1546.   Itm. receyvyd in money y^t ye Lorde gathered
      in Wytson Hollidays   -   -   -   -   xiij^s iiij^d

      Itm. p^d to Hugh Cotteril for mendyn of the
      Lordes harowe †·   -   -   -   -   ij^d

1547.   Itm. reseved of Dynis Shepard for the
      getheringe of the lord at Whitsunday   -   -   xxvij^s ^{d}v

---

[*] I am indebted to my friend Frederick Goodyear, Esq., the highly esteemed
chief constable of the county, for kindly instituting inquiries for me on the
subject, and procuring for my use the copy of this curiosity of literature through
the willing aid of Mr. Superintendent Deakins of Lutterworth.

† Harowes-Arrows (Halliwell's " Archaic Dictionary ").

1556.   Charge—

    Itm. J. Thom^s Postarn charge me R^d of John
Feshpole and Thom^s Maye yt their children
gathered in the towne at Whitsontyde and of
Steven Thorneton y^t he gethred ye same yere
beyng lorde of mysse rule -   -   -   v^{ll} xix^s viij^d

    Itm. R^d of bertylmew schaw yt he getherd
beying lorde at Est^r -   :   -   -   xx^s

    Itm. I R^d of Steven Schaw y^t he getherd &
hys company at Robin Hoods playe ij yeres -   xxix^s viij^d

    Itm. I R^d of John Hopkyns in p^{te} of Robyn
Hoods money -   -   -   -   -   v^s

    Itm. I R^d of Robert Holynsworth in p^{te} of y^e
money y^t hys son gethed at Whitsontide a^o 56 -   xxvj^s viij^d

    Itm. I R^d of Thom^a Richardson and Richard
Myln^r that they gatherd -   -   -   viij^s iij^d

            Sin.   xij^{ll} ix^s xj^d

1557.   Itm. R^d of Robert Hollyngwort of ye lords
money y^t was gathered att Wyssondery -   xlvj^s viij^d

    Itm. R^d at Wyssondery in oblasonnes -   vij^d vj^d ob.

    Itm. R^d of Robert Bocher for ye lords money
we Receved y^{tt} att Allhallowtyde -   -   ix^s ij^d

    Itm. R^d in ye overplusse of ye offerings of
the processions at Whitsonday -   -   -   xiij^d

1558.   Rec^d off ye offrynge ffor Melto att Whytson-
tyde -   -   -   -   -   -   viij^s iij^d

    Rec^d off the lord offe myssrulle -   -   xv^s

1559.   The Reckonyng and Accompt of me Xpor Why thed for
money receavyd the xxij day of May A^o 1559 the lordes
money at Easter and Whytsonday A^o ut supra as herewth
more playnly apperythe—

    I charge me reacevyd of the lords money
at Easter & at Whitsontide A^o 1559 S^m lj^s ob^d

Itm. R^d of Mr Payte for stone that he toke

ROBIN

out of the ffyelde　　-　　　-　　　-　　　-　　　xij^d　HOOD'S

PLAY.

To^{ll} of this my charge　　-　　　-　　　-　　lij^s ob^d

[The above money was expended in repairing the bridges and causeways of the town.]

1563. This is the Reckoning and Accompt of me Robt Odam Junior, being chosen and nomynated the Lorde at Melton at Whitsondaye A^o 1563 to gather the Devocyon of the Towne and Cuntrye wch is to be bestowed for the Repayring & mending the highe wayes, charge :—

Impmis R^d of Hawe [Holy] Thorsday at the chosinge of the Lorde and Ladye　　-　　'　-　　xviij^s x^d

Itm. at the gatheriuge of the malt and whete *　-　　-　　-　　-　　-　　-　　xviij^s

Itm. of Whitson Mondaye　　-　　　-　　　-　　xxv^s iij^d

Itm. of Tewsdaye　　-　　　-　　　-　　　-　　xxj^s v^d

Itm. of Wednesdaye　-　　　-　　　-　　　-　　xliij^s

Itm. of Thorsdaye　　-　　　-　　　-　　　-　　xj^d

To^{ll} charge　-　　　-　　　-　　　-　　　-　　v^{ll} x^s xj^d

Discharge (*inter alia*) :—

Itm. to the pip. (piper) † of hawe Thorsdaye　xij^d

Itm. for spyce for the cakes　-　　　-　　　-　　xxj^d

Itm. to the iiij foote men　　-　　　-　　　-　　viij^s

Itm. to the ij buttlers　-　　'　-　　　-　　　xx^d

Itm. for neyles to the lordes hall　　-　　　-　　ij^d

* For the Whitsun Ales. See Brand's "Popular Antiquities," etc.

† "Tom the Piper" was a well-known character in the May games. He is thus mentioned by Drayton, in his third "Eclogue " :—

"Myself above Tom Piper to advance,
Who so bestirs him in the Morris Dance,
For penny wage."

In the woodcut on the title page of " Kemp's Nine Daies Wonder : Performed in a Morrice from London to Norwich " (1600), Will Kemp's attendant, Thomas Slye, is represented in this character, with pipe, tabor stick and tabour ; and the coloured frontispiece to the second volume of Knight's " Old England," copied from a painted window, represents this and the other figures in an ancient Morris-dance.

ROBIN
HOOD'S
PLAY.

Itm. to Thom^s Kenne for bylding the lordes
hall * and mending a borde & vj. tressells   -   vij^d

Itm. to bartillmewe Allan for playing of
thorsday in Whitson weeke   -   -   -   vj^d

Itm. a pottell of Wyne for my lady Attredde   viij^d

Itm. iu cakes for her -   -   -   -   iiij^d

Item. to Rayne browne for bringing the
gowne from the launde †   -   -   -   vj^d

Itm. to Willm. Madder for playing iij dayes -   v^s iiij^d

Item. to Denys Shepard for pots   -   -   j^d

Item. to Nycobys Swashe for dressing my
lords horse, for breyd, & for his paynes   -   xiiij^d

Item. to John Downes for iiij^c (cccc) lyveryes ‡
& the payntine of ij staves   -   -   -   ij^s iiij^d

Item. for vij chickens for my lady Perin   -   xviij^d

[The remainder of the account consists of numerous pay-

---

* In the account of the churchwardens of St. Helen's, Abingdon (" Archæo-
logia," vol. i. p. 24), for the year 1556, there is an entry, " For setting up Robin
Hood's Bower ; " this, like the " lordes' hall " at Melton, was probably a wooden
booth or framework, covered with green boughs. Philip Stubs, in his rare book,
entitled " The Anatomie of Abuses " (London, 1585, f. 92 b.), gives a highly
curious description of the " Lorde of Misserule " and his attendants.   He says,
" Aboute the churche they goe again and againe, and so forthe into the churche-
yard, where they have commonly their *sommer haules, their Bowers, Arbours,*
and Banquettyng Houses set up, wherein they feast, banquet, and daunce all
that daie, and (peradventure) all that night too.   And thus these terrestrial
furies spend their Sabbaoth daie."   The " lorde's hall " at Melton was doubtless
of the same kind and for the same purpose.

† Laundre. a laundress (Halliwell's " Archaic Dictionary ").

‡ These " liveries " were badges formed of paper satin or other material, with
some device thereon, which were distributed among the spectators.   Thus, among
the entries in the " Northumberland Household Book " (quoted by Ritson, vol. i.
p. ciii.), we have the following :—

    " 15 C of leveres for Robin Hode -   -   -   -   -   0   5   0
    For leveres, paper, and sateyn   -   -   -   -   -   0   0 20."

ments for labour, stone, &c., for the repairs of highways and
bridges]

> Kelly's "Notices of Leicester," pp. 63-67.
>
> *See* "Folk-Lore," vol. ii. p. 330.
>
> *See also* Nichols' "Leicestershire," II., 248, quoting
> from the sermon of Latimer, who, going to
> preach at a certain town (probably Melton),
> was informed : "Sir, this is a holiday* with us ;
> we cannot hear you ; it is Robin Hood's Day.
> The parish are gone abroad to gather for Robin
> Hood." *See also* Nichols, III., 1008. Ed.

---

* In the original " busy day." *See also* Ritson's " Lytell Geste of Robin
Hode " (ed. Gutch, 1847), p. 106. Ed.

Part IV

FOLK-SAYINGS.

(a.)—JINGLES, NURSERY RHYMES, RIDDLES, &c.

JINGLES.   *Formulas.*—When goodies are distributed.

> "One's none, Two's some,
>   Three's a many,
>   Four's a penny (or a plenty, a flush, or a mort),
>   Five's a little hundred."

Northall, p. 334.
Evans, p. 190.

> "Chiffchaff, never change again,
>   As long as the world stands.   Amen."

"Leicestershire and Shropshire schoolboy formula solemnly ratifying an exchange of property."

Northall, p. 335.
Evans, p. 120.

Street Cries.—See an article by Mr. F. T. Mott, in "Bygone Leicestershire," p. 244.

(b)—PROVERBS.

(1.)—Anthropological.

" Different people have different 'pinions,
  Some like apples, and some like inions."

                                    Northall, p. 285.
                                    Evans, p. 176.

" If all the waters was wan sea,
  And all the trees was wan tree,
  And this here tree was to fall into that there sea,
  Moy, surs ! what a splish-splosh there'd be ! "

                                    Northall, p. 285.

A common rhyme usually considered an effective rebuke to
dealers in fanciful hypotheses.

                                    Evans, p. 252.

" *Aw* makes Dun draw."

                                    Evans, p. 94.

[Cf. Shakespeare, *Romeo and Juliet*, i. 4 : " If thou art dun,
we'll draw thee from the mire." *To draw dun out of the mire* was
a Christmas gambol or rural pastime.   Ed.]

" ' A plenty's better nur a floosh,' as o'd Bendigo Bilson said,
when the yoong masster gen 'im a change o' rabbit shot i' the
leg."

                                    Evans, p. 202.

" Soon crooks the tree, that good gambrel would be."

                                    Evans, p. 157.

" I've jobbed that job, as the woman said when she jobbed her
eye out."

                                    Evans, p. 178.

PROVERBS.   " You thought a lig
                                     Like Hudson's pig."

" If it is asked, 'And what did Hudson's pig think?' the
correct answer is 'Whoy, a thowt as they was a-gooin' to kill
'un, an' they oon'y run a ring threw it nooze.' "

                                                    Evans, p. 185.
                                                    Northall, p. 297.

"Good ale is meat, drink, and lodging."

                                                    Ray, p. 1.
                                                    Evans, p. 299.

" He has gone over Astordby Bridge backwards."   Spoken of
one that is past learning.

                                                    Ray, p. 317.
                                                    Evans, p. 299.

    Grose, p. 76, has Ass fordby Bridge.
                            [Query, the Pons Asinorum?   Ed.]

" A blot's no blot till it's hot." (*i.e.* hit.)

                                                    Ray, p. 103.
                                                    Evans, p. 300.

" What have I to do with Bradshaw's windmill? " (*i.e.* with
other men's matters.)

                                                    Grose, p. 76.
                                                    Ray, p. 248.
                                                    Evans, p. 300.

" A man must hold a candle to the Devil at times."

                                                    Evans, p. 300.
                                        Cf. Shakspeare, *Romeo and Juliet*, I., iv.

" 'Do as I say an' not as I do,' says the paa'son, or, 'as the
paa'son said when they whelt 'd 'im hum in a wheel-barra.' "

                                                    Evans, p. 300.

" Kaw me, and I'll kaw thee."

                                                    Evans, p. 302.

" He was hanged as spilt good liquor."

Evans, p. 302.

Red Bull-calf.—" ' He blushes like a red bull calf.' Ray has ' to blush like a black dog,' with the same significance. The phrase was once casually used in my hearing, and I was moved to ask when it was that the red bull-calf had blushed ? ' A nivver blooshed but wanst,' said Sam, ' an' that wur laast Moonday wur a wile, when Kimbulin's mule called 'im bahsta'd.' "

Evans, p. 300.

" The same again, quoth Mark of Belgrave."

Ray, 248.   Evans, p. 299.   Grose, p. 76.
Scott, " Heart of Midlothian," ch. xxix.

Var.   Mark of Makfield.

" Hobbadehoy, neither man nor boy."

Evans, p. 301.

" Kissing goes by favour."

Evans, p. 302.

" Last makes fast."

Evans, p. 302.

" Let them laf as lewses, for them as wins weell laf."

Evans, p. 302.

" One good turn deserves another."

Evans, p. 302.

" One yate for another, good fellow."

Evans, p. 302.

" An empty sack won't stand upright."

Evans, ·p. 303.

" Service is no inheritance."

Evans, p. 303.

" Never speak ill of the bridge that carries you."

Evans, p. 303.

" Speak of a man as you find him."

Evans, p. 303.

PROVERBS.   " Tell-tale tit ! your tongue shall be slit
             And every dog in all the town shall have a little bit."

Evans, p. 303.

" A thump on the back with a stone."

Evans, pp. 273, 303.

" Him as looked at the staas fell i' the doyke, but him as
looked at the graound foon' a poose."

Evans, p. 256.

" Yo' goo wum an' toy oop Oogly ! "

Evans, p. 281.

" Ah would'nt call the king my ooncle."

Evans, p. 281.

" ' Shay's as nasty as a devil unknobbed ' (*i.e.* a devil who has
either never had any knobs fastened on his horns or else has
succeeded in getting rid of them).   The phrase well illustrates
the bovine character of the popular ' devil.' "

Evans, p. 282.

" Better have the Quane to yer aant nur the King to yer
ooncle."

Evans, p. 282.

" Gin him the whetstun ! If a doon't shaa'p his sen a bit, a
woona git out a sooch another afoor Tewsd'y wik."

Evans, p. 288.

Simples.—" A'd ought to be coot for the simples," is a phrase
implying that the person spoken of is a fool. The metaphor,
probably incorrectly, regards folly as a curable disease, and
suggests that the patient should be " cut," *i.e.* lanced, so as to
allow the perilous stuff to escape.

Evans, p. 240.

" Thou art *like unto like,* as the devill said to the Collyar."   Saying of a Leicestershire woman charged against her in a deposition
before the Justices, dated 19th May, 1603.

" Hall Papers," vol. xxi.

(2) Physical Proverbs.

Mists.—

"If Belvoir hath a cap
You churls of the vale look to that."

"When mist doth rise from Belvoir Hole,
O, thou be sure the weather's foul."

> Northall, p. 39.
> Evans, p. 300.
> Burton, p. 2.
> Grose, p. 75.
> Inwards, p. 100.

"When Bardon Hill has a cap,
Hay and grass will suffer for that."

> Leicestershire N. and Q., iii., 160.

Fishing.—

"When the wind's in the east
The fishes bite least,
When the wind's in the north
The fishes won't come forth,
When the wind's in the south
It blows the bait in the fishes' mouth."

> Northall, p. 279.
> Evans, p. 301.

East Wind.—

"If the winds i' th' East of Easter Dee,
You'll ha' plenty o' grass but little good hee."

> Northall, p. 451.
> Evans, p. 169.

Rain.—

"Hark! I hear the asses bray,
We shall have some rain to-day."

> (Rutland) Northall, p. 472.
> Inwards, p. 127.

PROVERBS.   *Christmas.*—

> " A green Christmas brings a heavy harvest."

> (Rutland) Inwards, p. 38.

Moon.—

> " Saturday change and Sunday full
> Niver did good and niver wull."

> Evans, p. 293.

Bees.—

> " A swarm of bees in May
> Is worth a load of hay :
> A swarm of bees in June
> Is worth a silver spoon :
> A swarm of bees in July
> Is not worth a fly."

> Evans, p. 299.

Seasons and Death.—

> " March will sarch,
> An' Epril troy,
> But Mee will see,
> If ye live or doy."

> Evans, p. 230.

Shifting.—" ' Thray shifts are as bad as a fire,' *i.e.* three removals from one house to another.".

> Evans, p. 237.

> " When the ice before Martlemas bears a duck
> Then look for a winter o' mire and muck."

> Evans, p. 191.
> Northall, p. 455.

" ' To rain by planets,'—said of rain that comes down partially, wetting one field and leaving another close adjoining quite dry. ' But why by planets, my friend,' asked I. ' Why, don't you know,' said my informant, ' it's all along o' the planets.' "

> Evans, p. 214 and 303.

"Snow at Candlemass
Stops to handle us."

(Rutland) "Folk-Lore Record," iv., p. 127.

Inwards, p. 14.

"If birds begin to whistle in January, frost's to come."

(Rutland) Inwards, p. 10.

(3) HISTORICAL PROVERBS.

Sir John Talbot of Swannington.—A lane and wood near Whitwick are still called by this name, and the following couplet is a common proverb there :—

> "Nought remains of Talbot's name
> But Talbot Wood and Talbot Lane."

Potter, p. 155.

Among those whose names are fossilized in the local nomenclature, Sir John Talbot of Swannington may also claim a place—the gigantic knight who died in 1365, and lies under an equally gigantic effigy in Whitwick Church. A local distich, hardly to be called a rhyme, thus moralizes over his topographical celebrity :—

> "Talbot wood and Talbot lane
> Is all that's left of Talbot's name."

Evans, p. 43.

[*See* Nichols, III., 1122. Ed.]

Hastings.—"He is none of the Hastings." Spoken of a slow person. There is an equivoque in the word Hastings, which is the name of a great family in Leicestershire, which were Earls of Huntington. They had a fair house at Ashby-de-la-Zouch, now much ruined.

Ray, 196, quoted by Evans, p. 301.

[Grose, p. 92, has the proverb of Sussex, and says it is an allusion to the pea called hastings, because the earliest of its kind. Ed.]

(c.) NICKNAMES, PLACE RHYMES, &c.

Bean belly Leicestershire.— . . . . from the great plenty of that grain grown there. " Shake a Leicestershire man by the collar, and you shall hear the beans rattle in his belly."

> Ray, p. 247. Evans, p. 299. Burton, p. 32. Nichols, IV., p. 518.
>
> [" But those yeomen smile at what is said to rattle in their bellies, whilst they know good silver ringeth in their pockets." Fuller. Ed.]
>
> [*See* " Bygone Leicestershire," p. 106, where *Fuller* and *Drayton* are quoted. *Also* " Folk-Lore Journal" iii., pp. 83 and 85. Ed.]

Shake a Leicestershire woman by the petticoat, and the beans will rattle in her throat.

> Southey's " Commonplace Book," 4th Series, 1851, p. 341, quoting "St. James' Magazine," 1762, vol. ii., p. 13.

See " Local Customs." Mayor of Leicester (Rex Fabarum).
Rutland Raddleman.

> Drayton, Polyolbion, xxiii., 263. Grose, p. 88. Ray, p. 259.

*Tin-hat Hinckley.—*This is a common nickname but its origin appears to be unknown.

> *See* under " Festival Customs " [Whitsuntide Procession at Hinckley] for the germs of a possible explanation. Ed.

Groby Pool.—" Then I'll thatch Groby Pool with Pancakes" is given in Ray's book, but there is no explanation. It was intended as a reply to a braggart who was boasting of doing some wonderful thing. The leaf of the water-lily, of which there used to be many in the pool. bears, when in decay, a resemblance to a pancake.

J.

> " Leicestershire N. and Q.," vol. i., 280, and vol. ii., 15. Grose, p. 76.
> Evans, p. 301.

[*See* Sir W. Scott, "Heart of Midlothian," chap. xxix.,
and Carlyle, "Past and Present," book iii., chap. i.
It is used to denote the impossible. " I hope there's
nae bad company on the road, sir?" asked
Jeanie. "Why, when it's clean without them,
I'll thatch Groby Pool with pancakes." Scott,
l. c. Ed.]

Groby Pool.—"For his death there is many a wet eye in Groby
Pool."

Ray. p. 248.
Grose, p. 77.

"When a doys thee'll ba wet oys i' Grewby Pule."

Evans, p. 301.

Old Saying.—Time was when those bare hills (of Charnwood
Forest), as well as the valleys at their feet, were covered with
majestic oaks—when, to use the words of an old tradition, " a
squirrel might be hunted six miles without once touching the
ground ; and when a traveller might journey from Beaumanor
to Bardon, on a clear summer's day, without seing the sun."

"History and Antiquities of Charnwood Forest."
T. R. Potter, 1842, p. 5.
[*See* " Folk-Lore Handbook," p. 165. Ed.]

" In and out,
Like Bellesdon, I wot."

Grose, p. 77.
Ray, p. 248.
Evans, p. 300.
Northall, p. 39.

" In and out,
Like Billsdon Brook."

Nichols, II., p. 436.

Loseby.—This name gave rise to a rustic proverb of the country :
when a man sells a thing for less than he hoped to get for it he
says, " I must e'en be content to go home by Loseby (it)."

Nichols, III., p. 337.

2 s

" Brentingley pancheons
　　And Wyfordby pans,
　　Stapleford organs,
　　And Burton tingtangs."
　　　　　　" North Church Bells of Leicestershire," p. 284.
　　　　　　　　　　　　　　　　　Northall, p. 40.

" Bread for borough men;
　At Great Glenn
　There are more great dogs than honest men."
　　　　　　　　　　　　　　Grose, p. 75.
　　　　　　　　　　　　　　Ray, p. 248.
　　　　　　　　　　　　　　Evans, pp. 300, 301.

　　" Go to Sketchley."
　　See under " Holy Wells."

　　　" Higham on the Hill
　　　　Stoke in the Vale,
　　　Wykin for buttermilk,
　　　　Hinckley for ale."
　　　　　　　　　　　　　Northall, p. 40.
　　　　　　　　　　　　　Nichols, IV., p. 677.

　" Mountsorrel he mounted at
　　Rodely (Rothley) he rode by,
　　Onelip (Wanlip) he leaped o'er,
　　At Birstall he burst his gall,
　　At Belgrave he was buried at."

　This relates to an exploit of the giant Bell and his wonderful
sorrel horse.
　　　　　　　　　　　　　　　　Northall, p. 40.

　There is a Leicestershire proverb :
　　" He leaps like a Bell giant or devil of Mount Sorrel."
　　　　　　　　　　　　　　Grose, p. 76.
　　　　　　　　　　　　　　Northall, p. 40.

　　See also under " Place Legends."

" We must dew as the' dew at Quorn
    What we don't dew to dee, we must dew i' the morn." *

> Northall, p. 41.
> Evans, p. 303.

" The last man as he killed
    Keeps pigs in Hinckley field."

> Grose, p. 76.

Said of a boaster. Quoted by Ray, as is also, " I'll throw you in Harborough field : " to which he appends the explanation, " A threat for children ; Harborough having no field."

> Ray, p. 248, *ibid.* p. 292. Evans, pp. 148 and 301.
> Northall, p. 292. Grose, p. 75.

[The proverb now runs " A goose will eat all the grass that grows in Harborough field," and it is so given by Burton, p. 128. Ed.]

> " Thorpe Arnold, four people,
>   Leather bells, wooden steeple."

Hog's Norton.—" Hog's Norton, where Pigs play on the organ." The true name of the town, according to Peck, is Hock's Norton, and one Piggs, Ray's man so-called,† was the organist of the parish church. Possibly ; but the name has a mythic air, and to say that a man comes from Hog's Norton is simply equivalent to saying that he snores. The distinctive name of the village was probably derived from a Danish ancestor of the good Leicestershire stock of " Hooke."

> Grose, p. 76.
> Evans, p. 301.

[*See* Sir T. Cave's explanation in Nichols, IV. 849*. Ed.]

* " We'll do as they do at *Quern.*
    What we do not to-day, we must do in the morn."
> Ray's " Proverbs," fourth edition, 1768, p. 62.

† " Pigs play on the organs. A man so called at Hog's Norton in Leicestershire, or Hock's Norton."—*Ray.*

Hose and Long Clawson.—" There are more whores in Hose than honest women in Long Clawson." The pun is double-barrelled, the " honest women in Long Clawson " being a sufficiently near approximation to " honestwomen in long clothes " to satisfy the requirements of a local joke.

> Evans, p. 302.   Grose, p. 76.

Lockington Wake.—"Put up your pipes, and go to Lockington Wake."

> Grose, p. 75.   Ray, p. 248.

I suppose it is equivalent to "Go to Bath."

> Evans, p. 302.

An Uppingham trencher.   (*Rutland.*)

> Grose, p. 88.   Ray, p. 259.   Evans, p. 303.

" A Leicester Plover, and that's a bag-pudding."

> Scott, "Heart of Midlothian," chap. xxxii.   Grose, p. 77.   Evans, p. 302.

" Stretton i' th' street
   Where shrews meet."   (*Rutland.*)

> Grose, p. 88.   Ray, p. 259.   Evans, p. 303.

Carlton Wharlers.—Camden tells us that " almost all the natives of this town (Carlton Curlieu) by a peculiarity of the soil or water, or some other unknown natural cause, speak in a dissonant, inarticulate, manner, drawing their words with great harshness out of their throats, and labouring under a kind of wharling." *

> Nichols, II., p. 544.   (He also quotes Burton, Fuller, Brome, and Bishop Gibson.)
> Burton, p. 67-68.   Grose, p. 75.

---

* *Rhotacismus.*—Gongh's Camden, vol. ii.. p. 193.

The " Carlton Wharlers " mentioned by Camden may perhaps have been immigrants from Cumberland or some other northern county, who formed a settlement at Carlton Curlieu.

Evans, p. 1.

> [" The good folks of Berwick ' owing to some occult cause,' as funny old Fuller expresses it, ' have a wharling in their throats, so that they cannot pronounce the letter R.' " Denham Tracts. Folk-Lore Society. 1892. I., p. 288. Ed.

Also published by Llanerch:

OLD SCOTTISH CUSTOMS
W. J. Guthrie

COUNTY FOLKLORE:
ORKNEY & SHETLAND
G F. Black

COUNTY FOLKLORE:
NORTHUMBERLAND
M. C. Balfour

LEGENDS FROM RIVER AND MOUNTAIN
Carmen Silva, Queen of Roumania

THE FOLKLORE OF PLANTS
T. F. Thiselton Dyer

THE FOLKLORE OF THE ISLE OF MAN
A. W. Moore

THE DAWN OF THE WORLD:
THE MEWAN INDIANS OF CALIFORNIA
C. Hart Merriam

BRITIAN'S LIVING FOLKLORE
Roy Palmer

For a complete list of c.200 small-press editions and
facsimile reprints, write to Llanerch Publishers,
Felinfach, Lampeter, Dyfed, SA48 8PJ.